THE DENTIST'S

UNFAIR

ADVANTAGE

VOLUME 2

An indepth discussion of the key tenets of ethical selling and promotion in use in the most successful dental practices.

DR. JAMES R. MCANALLY

ISBN: 0989111504
ISBN 13: 9780989111508

Contents

Key Tenet #13
Understand the Concept of Real-World Readiness

Key Tenet #14
Use Systems to Shorten Patient Buying
and Decision-Making Time

Key Tenet #15
To Reach Those Who Aren't Ready
"Right Now," Use Follow-Up Systems

Key Tenet #16
Follow-Up Never Ends

Key Tenet #17
Proclaim Yourself the "Wizard" and
Create a Category of One

Key Tenet #18
Your Staff Must Believe in You as
the Expert and Wizard

Key Tenet #19
Use Staff Time (Group or Individual) to Focus on
Prospective Cases; Otherwise, the Ceiling
of Complexity Damages Success

Key Tenet #20
Rehearse and Practice Your Ethical
Selling System Consistently

Preface

We live in a world where consultants, coaches, and teachers—especially when it comes to marketing and sales (i.e. "case acceptance")—are frequently not highly successful doers or, more important, doers willing to share their successes *and* their mistakes with those who seek the same results.

That's where I draw the line.

Not only do I consult, coach, and teach other dentists, but I've enjoyed significant success in these endeavors, maintained a highly successful clinical practice and a consulting and sales business. I study—as well as innovate and apply—what science has to offer in the realms of clinical treatment, marketing, business, and sales of all of the above.

The results for me, and for those who train in the Master Dentists Academy Programs using our materials related to marketing and ethical selling, include the following:

- Dramatically improve patients' appearance
- Restore ability to function comfortably
- Eradicate chronic pain
- Help people look and feel younger
- Increase case acceptance for every type of case and every 'style' of practice

- Allow many doctors to choose a professional life where they are compensated fairly for their skill, receive additional respect from peers, and enjoy a great profession even more

For those clinicians with the most skills and training, it means more cases where accident, disease, and neglect caused patients to virtually give up hope are now being treated in almost every type of economy and location around the world.

In this book, you will find the terms "Ethical Selling" and "dental case acceptance" used interchangeably. In a perfect world, they would be the same; however, in the broader profession and outside of those dentists with training in the subject matter they are not. Take a critical look at the mail crossing your desk, and you'll notice improved "acceptance" promised as a byproduct of an endless list of random subject matter ranging from clinical courses and even applied to pieces of equipment. Few of the things with this benefit attached deliver the result desired.

If you happen to find a course related to selling professional services, the day or half-day is spent attempting to memorize selling-related phrases that are impossible to remember and invariably feel more at home on a used-car lot. These courses promise that selling can be a staff-only event without the doctor needing to do anything, essentially removing the captain/coach/general (e.g., leader) from the ship/team/army. How smart is *that*?

The reader will likely hear, mixed in with these ineffective promises to improve case acceptance, one of the greatest lies from the podium or pages of a trade magazine that "every patient can afford any type of dentistry—they just need to want it more." Those who have practiced a long time know from experience that this statement is untrue. I've yet to meet a colleague who couldn't relate plenty of stories of patients who did want dental services but were not in the financial situation to make the investment.

While most of what "case acceptance" gets attached to has little to do with delivering the desired result, those seeking to learn to "ethically sell" understand that only through psychology and behavioral science, applied to trainable, systematic (repeatable!) steps, is real success possible for ongoing, acceptable percentages of patients accepting treatment.

The best news is that a structured system for Ethical Selling is attainable and a highly predictable choice for any team and doctor who wants a career-long foundation in such. Via Ethical Selling, practices routinely get the fees compensatory to their care, skill, and judgment and they help more patients opt for better services. Beyond better fees and having patients make better choices related to their dental care, they also improve the results of existing or new marketing. Finally, a foundational in ethical selling your best services is the key to escaping from or preventing every being caught in the commodity trap of insurance dictated discounting in which many in the profession ensnared. *If at any time while studying this book, you feel that Ethical Selling and a check-list approach for consultations and treatment presentations makes sense for you and your team and you want formal training in such, you'll find two special invitations preceding this section to help you get started.*

The book is split into two volumes. Volume 1 is designed to create a better understanding of the fundamentals related to promoting one's services based on human characteristics that are as true now as when the first "billboard" postings were erected in the Middle Ages.

Volume 2, which is in your hand, explores in detail The 39 Key Tenets necessary for private practice success in an economy where demographics of dental disease, how dentistry gets paid for, and the economics of the middles classes have shifted away from the previous model that the profession grew accustomed to. These Tenets when present in a practice, lead to patients making better decisions about the best dentistry available at any time. Most of these tenets will be as applicable now as they will in fifty years when technology has evolved and things we couldn't imagine will be used by clinical practices. These key tenets are incorporated into the training materials, programs, and promotional materials dispensed to our Academy members.

After reading volume 2, you will understand the following:

- What motivates patients the most, regardless of opinions on whether or not it is rational

- The most important concept to keep in mind when thinking about promoting the services you focus on in your practice

- The reality of the types of patients presenting to any practice

- How to have patients understand what you wish to discuss

- The missing step that practices forget even when making significant investments in external advertising

- Key aspects of case presentation that affect at least 50 percent of your acceptance rate

- Specific directions on how to present options and fees

- Which people, and how many, need to be at presentations of proposed treatment

Introduction

"Experience is what you get when you don't get what you want."

Let's start by first answering the question that many will have which is "why the title of The Dentists Unfair Advantage?"

Firstly, I selected the title to intentionally repel those dentists who after reading such would not be curious to the matters discussed herein. Curiosity cannot arise until there is awareness that something exists and I have little doubt that this title will create an awareness for many clinicians to become curious and as a result read the important subject matter discussed in these pages. It's doubtful that the clinician who would not become curious after reading the title would be interested in such topics beyond the mechanics of "drilling and filling" teeth regardless of how much the tenets discussed may impact patient choice and behavior.

Furthermore, the title was chosen to illustrate that words matter a lot, be they for promoting one's practice or for titles of non-clinical books, since word choice affects interest.

I have no tolerance for those who refuse to acknowledge the impact non-clinical topics affect a patient deciding to call a practice and present to an appointment because of an ad and how specific sequences of steps followed by the doctor and team result in patients making the best decision possible for their situation with the resources they have.

While many dentists are challenged by economic, de-mographic, and reimbursement structure changes, those embracing non-clinical behavioral science, and working to apply it, perform more of the services they enjoy, and have more patients who are thankful for their professional help.

Lastly the title was picked so that an important message would have a better chance of being delivered to a wider audience since every reader pulled into the discussion of these concepts would also receive a firm grounding in the concept of "fairness."

Here's a news flash. Life is not fair. Except for those statisti-cally lucky few born into immense wealth, life is a one hun-dred percent certified *unfair* deal.

If you happen to have been born in one of the relatively free societies, where your day is protected by the rule of law, you can say that you are one of the luckiest on the planet. US-born dentists are forewarned that from your corner there shall be no whining related to the even luckier circumstanc-es allotted to you simply by your location of birth!

Life is unfair from the first cry, and it's made more so by changing economics, even in the "land of opportunity." Unfair is a reality, so it's either go through life complaining or acknowledge the truth and, most important, move on to do something about your circumstances.

Because life begins, continues, and ends with little of it being fair, we are all tasked with finding *advantages* in our endeavors that *reduce the unfairness* in our individual realities.

- The following short list of questions will stimulate more thoughts by you on what is fair and not surrounding your personal circumstance in practice:

- Is it fair that the practitioner competes with massive corporations who have unlimited marketing budgets to influence what consumers purchase; including many products that are unhealthy and damage the body or pollute the environment?

- Is it fair that the *exact same* dental supplies, devices, and equipment can vary in cost by 200-300% based solely on country of residence?

- Is it fair that in certain markets, a dental benefits administering company can have a de facto monopoly?

- Is it fair that dental "insurance" payments are paid differently simply on zip code of a practice location?

- Is it fair that dental education results in massive debts?

- Is it fair that occupations in which money is simply pushed around between large banks and risked in high stakes bets can result in massive financial windfalls for those skilled at such or in public financial bailouts when their efforts fall flat?

- Is it fair that employers don't typically recognize the value in dental benefits for every producing employee?

- Is it fair that most patients can't afford to purchase or won't purchase health services that are beneficial and impact quality of daily life?

- Is it fair that government reimbursement programs consider dentistry non-essential health-care?

This book could be filled with nothing but lists of items, like the above, that most practitioners would point to as things that are "unfair" to them personally, to their business, and to humanity at large.

It is <u>only</u> via an ongoing and intentional *accumulation of advantages* via education, experience, or through the experience and knowledge of others that you can consistently *reduce the unfairness* you are confronted with every day. *You have a choice to accumulate advantages on an ongoing basis that make your life a lot less unfair or complain.*

For definition purposes, "unfair advantages for dentists are *those advantages gained over time that directly reduce the inherent unfairness of practice and business realities of professional practice and are derived from different ways of thinking and communicating to patients and prospective patients as well as a direct side effect of having better systems to operate the business of your practice as compared to other dentists.*"

Dentists who have these accumulated advantages are often visible in their practice area because they heavily promote their services and they often promote differently than other dentists based on their knowledge of human behavior. While others might try to copy what is visible externally in these practices (believing that surely that's the "secret"), the real advantage is what happens inside the practice, how communication happens, and how patients are treated personally by the doctor and team. The unfair advantage is akin to plumbing, buried inside a building, that only those on the inside understand—and almost impossible to copy by a direct competitor.

Most in the profession think that advantages are derived only from clinical skills and the pursuit of more clinical skills. Yes, clinical skills are one part of accumulating advantages, but much like operating systems in computers, their maintenance and upgrading are a fact and must occur on a constant basis. Patients believe that practitioners are competent and interchangeable regardless of how many certificates they have on the wall, which negates what most dentists feel is their main advantage!

The accumulation of advantages that greatly reduce the unfairness that impacts practice is accessible to anyone with a license, only a small number will seek such accumulation on a consistent basis; it requires a realization that these advantages exist, can be acquired, and requires *effort and ongoing work.* The concepts and strategies in this book provide direct roadmaps to creating and achieving advantages that will help you on a daily basis with dealing with the unfairness you confront!

My Experience

I've experienced both sides of the equation: having no advantages and having them in abundant supply. Being in clinical dentistry for almost a quarter of a century, I can attest that for at least 50 percent of my time directly treating patients, I had no advantage in the market place. During those times, the value of what I brought to the market and to patients was a lot less, and it showed financially as well as in the decisions my patients made.

While I did well by average dentist standards, I earned less on an hourly basis and saw patients to the point of unhealthy exhaustion. During those lean times, I did fewer of the procedures I enjoyed and did them at fees that weren't fair to me, or my team, for the investment it took to get my title and create a team. The worst part of that period was the fact that as a consequence of not having an unfair advantage, I underserved the community of patients around my practice. Practices with fewer accumulated advantages have fewer patients choosing to restore disease and it fails to serve as many patients as it could.

I was blind to the realities of what patients wanted from me and did not know what mattered when it came to promoting and advertising. I did not offer choices in ways that mattered to the patient (and which would evolve into our check-list system for Ethical Selling and help patients make the best decisions possible).

For the other 50 percent of my clinical career, through a lot of time investing in consulting services—the best of which were not related to dentistry, moving past "average" dentist mindset and thinking, and via expensive personal testing—I found the advantages that dealt with the unfairness issues that confront modern practices.

As a result, more patients found their way to my door to receive great dental services that changed their lives and restored lost quality of life.

While behaviorists are still unraveling brain chemistry and environmental elements that contribute to happiness, at least one part of happiness relates to smiling, so my advantages accumulated to deal with unfairness also elevated the happiness factor for more patients.

The advantages also meant a lot of implant cases, reconstructions, dental sedation, and, my all-time favorite, cosmetic dentures. Many dentists are qualified to do these procedures and more, but are marooned without enough advantages to counter the unfair reality that most patients can't or won't purchase their services. A lack of accumulated advantages holds them back and makes for drudgery.

More on Fairness

Is it fair that one dentist can choose to have a much more enjoyable and profitable practice than another degree holder across the street who, from a technical standpoint of skill, probably isn't that much different?

As a professional, which scenario would you prefer? Would it be the one where you have advantages or the one without? Everyone who has "been there, done that" will agree that the version of practice, where the advantages work to their benefit and create fairness for them personally has a long list of benefits.

How does this (accumulation of advantages) happen?

Perhaps 20 percent of the advantage is the mix of clinical services (and a largest component of this involves being a painless dentist). Eighty percent is related to the messages put into the market place, the steps your team and you are trained to take and, just as important, what not to do in your interactions with patients.

Many of the advantages arise from a different understanding of promoting services, and more important, that specific steps are involved to remove as many unknowns from treatment discussions as possible.

Can this kind of a shift in reality happen overnight? Certainly not, although the learning curve is faster today should you make the important choices to address the non-clinical things that lead to advantages that greatly impact your service business.

In practical terms, your practice and team can see benefits from as little as a few hours of training to be introduced to Ethical

DR. JAMES R. MCANALLY   ◆   THE DENTIST'S UNFAIR ADVANTAGE

Selling and master the Ethical Selling process and the check-list system taught at a leisurely pace over six to twelve months. Building permanent, advantages throughout the practice's systems can take several years, which is a small investment in a professional career that can now span forty years.

What's Required?

While some chronic physical limitations prevent my train-ing for endurance sports these days, I still like to use sport-ing analogies from my history in rowing, swimming, and triathlon (my three favorites) to help anyone contemplating undertaking endeavors that require a six-month to two-year investment to get an unfair advantage.

As an adult, I've completed a number of short- and long-distance rowing and triathlon events. They ranged from a few minutes of sprinting (a rowing race) or an hour crawl-ing across the San Francisco Bay (I swam from Alcatraz on five occasions) to a fourteen-hour Ironman triathlon. All of these experiences have commonalities (beyond pain, trips to the physiotherapist, and admittedly some obsessive be-havior), and they require the following:

- Plans (previously shown to work by others)
- Preparation
- Practice
- Coaching

These four items, tied to *desire,* allow almost anyone to do any of those sports at almost any age.

The same ingredients, added to desire, are needed to obtain and put into place the advantages discussed in this book

8

that give you more of what you want out of your practice and allow you to consistently overcome the unfairness of the marketplace and irrational behavior of your patients.. Getting your dental "unfair advantage" will require a lot less pain and destruction to your body than any sporting endeavor, and you'll have a higher level of personal and satisfaction, not to mention the additional patients who have their own stories and are impacted by what you can do for them.

Fortunately, most dentists and teams who will read these this book or dig in for specific and focused help are the ones who ask themselves, "Where can I get my advantages and get them *permanently?*"

It is in this spirit of conquering "unfairness" that I promise readers will receive, conceptually and from a practical strategy standpoint, insight on how to attain advantages that benefit their practice and patients.

About This Book

This volume contains key tenets that apply for practitioners who wish to increase their numbers of patients. Our Academy members use these principles in their daily routines and operations.

Many dentists will find what's discussed an eye-opening experience, and for some, it will fill in questions that they perhaps didn't even know to ask, much less find an answer for.

Most of the tenets are discussed in great detail conceptually, and enough structure is provided to implement them directly from the text.

Dentists who wish to benefit the most from these tenets will take what's contained here seriously, will change how they approach advertising messages, and will formalize their team's training in Ethical Selling to incorporate the relative tenets directly into their daily, weekly, and annual routines.

Key Tenet #1

Our Marketing Messages (Solutions) Must Match Our Patients Desires, Wants, or Needs (Problems)

This concept is probably the most underappreciated among dentists of all types when it comes to marketing for the cases they want and are trained to do.

Unless you want to waste time, energy, and money, every contact with potential patient must focus on solutions for the specific problems they are bothered by, be they sporadic or every day.

If you talk about the deepest disability, more patients (even those without serious problems) will know your services exist. Missing teeth is the ultimate motivator regardless of whether a patient is in dentures or not. Thus, we always poke, prod, and irritate the deepest disability of "toothlessness" and its consequences.

Google search statistics show that "dental implant" is out searched by "denture" by at least 500,000 searches per month! That is reason enough to "love the denture as your best friend" and realize we are *very* fortunate that it has such a feared and esteemed history and awareness in the public psyche. It is the oldest, most recognized, universally known, and most feared dental device in history.

While Google no longer shows total search volume, it provides snapshots based on long-term search volume to show relative numbers of search, languages, and search origins. Google's snapshot of the terms "Denture" versus "Dental Implant" consistently show that the searcher is more likely to start with the word "denture" first no matter when the snapshots have been taken. Patients do not begin searches with the terms that a dentist would type into the search bar. Not only does this matter in the online world but with the words presented to the public in marketing any service. The public will start with the basic dental words they know not the words you personally feel they should know. Google can serve as a research tool to help provide direction on what messages to use even in offline marketing based on what patients are typing into the search bar.

When it comes to your message of solutions to problems, it's also critical to keep in mind that you are not the target patient. You can never underestimate the need to make the message clear so that the majority of people understand what you are offering.

The average professional has an IQ of 120 while the majority of the population occupies the rest of the intelligence bell curve. If your message is understood by only those of equal or greater intelligence, you are bypassing lots of untreated reconstructive patients.

You may ask, "Yes, but what about money and intelligence? Surely, the smart patients are the ones with resources."

Several years ago, a twenty-five-year longitudinal study from a highly regarded Ohio State economist showed no meaningful statistical correlation between savings (money in the bank) and intelligence (Dr. Jay Zagorksy, Ohio State University, Journal of Intelligence). We must limit our message to a basic denominator that patients of below-average and average intelligences can understand. By doing so, we don't miss the opportunity to communicate more patients who may have the resources to benefit from services.

Taking all this into account, it's no wonder that dentures—wearing them, needing them, having to get them, fearing them—generates *the* best response for acquiring complex case patients. Patients of all intelligences know the term and it serves as the starting point that leads to many other procedures. Beyond the understandable terminology, the denture also intersects with another powerful human behavior which is loss, fear of loss, and loss avoidance.

No matter what service you would like to focus on, think about what problems the procedures solve, what losses it prevents, let Google show you the what terminology patients would use to look for this information and then develop your messages.

Key Tenet #2

Message Complexity Greatly Affects Promotional Results

Professionals easily get caught in fallacies of how "intelligent" promotional messages regarding services must be for the public at large to convey "quality" and competency of their services. There is an intelligence disconnect between understanding the difference between themselves as providers and the public as patients and consumers of services.

Emotional (practical) intelligence and general "IQ" are different types of intelligence measurements. From a general intelligence perspective, if the prospective patient can't understand a concept presented in a promotion about a solution, there's little chance of a next step occurring for choosing a service or practice.

Another common fallacy, related to intelligence and understanding, is the belief that by designing "intelligent" messages, the practitioner is more likely to find those interested in investing in their service and more likely to find those with greater financial means. This fallacy was debunked in Tenet 1 via discussion of Dr. Zagorsky's research.

The ultimate application is that all dental promotional messages must be understandable by *all* including those with average or below-average intelligence. If the message is too complex and as a result poorly understood, fewer patients respond and fewer patients benefit from needed services.

Key Tenet #3

Message Rotation Diminishes Results

Rosser Reeves, considered one of the fathers of "scientific advertising," conducted the foundational studies in the 1950's showing the limits of what consumers what consumers remembered; specifically when it came to how many claims could be made to the customer, how many claims could be remembered, and what happened when the messages about the claims were rotated.

In our age of overstimulation, distraction, and short attention spans, his data, derived from nearly fifty years of measurement by his teams, is even more applicable. Consumers had a difficult time remembering what claims were being made then as it related to a service or what a product was about when times were significantly less complex. In an age where a multitude of tasks and information compete with memory and awareness, ignoring these known functional limitations of the human mind is a serious mistake.

Napoleon was asked, at Saint Helena, the secret of his remarkable success in picking the marshals who led his armies. His answer was, "I did not pick them. They were selected by the God of Battles." The same holds true in our endeavors to find the correct balance of marketing (newsprint, Internet, radio, TV) that beckons patients needing your services to your front door. The "gods of phone calls/cases going forward" are the ultimate electors for which ads, locations, and frequencies are appropriate.

Memory Fades Quickly

Fifty years of data show that consumers (patients and prospective patients) forget quickly, and changing the story or message is the same as starting over.

At any time, a certain percentage of patients know your story. Six months later, the same percent knows the story, but half of them have forgotten it, and you've attracted a new group.

- Your story is forgotten unless it is endlessly repeated.

- If the story changes, understanding, comprehension, and retention (memory) of it drop.

- Running two competing messages at same time has the same consequences: patients remember one strong claim/concept.

- Changing an ad has same effect as starting over. Unless a service becomes outmoded, a great ad will not wear out. A great ad that stimulates those who are missing teeth won't die in effectiveness unless all the people missing teeth go away or unless a new procedure, widely understood by the consumers, has supplanted the old procedure. In reality, most consumers understand that "implant teeth" are superior to dentures, but they have no idea that cosmetic dentures or "facelift" dentures are better than "dentures."

Multiple Claims Fail

Reeves's concept of "one strong claim," backed by his data, is why a patient will remember one thing from your promotion—one strong claim or concept.

Here are a few problem-solution headlines that use the "one strong claim" effectively.

Teeth in an Hour
Teeth in a Day
STOPS Denture and Missing Tooth Problems
STOPS Tooth Loss
STOPS Dental Anxiety
STOPS Dental Pain
STOPS Teeth Embarrassment

Direct Applications

Keep your message about how you uniquely operate or practice simple and understandable.

Be careful with multiple claims, as they suck power from the main reason to call.

Limit your number of claims beyond the main one.

Tie any secondary claims back to the main claim.

Beware of claim "vampires." Reeves's "vampire" was anything creative and beautiful that didn't directly contribute to the one, strong message and would suck the result out of the money spent. Creative and beautiful are OK if they reinforce the main message. Today's marketing (dentists included) is full of vampires that don't strengthen a message. Promotional messages in which the vampire has been removed are invariably labeled "less imaginative" and don't win the awards that designers give each other. Advertising is designed for its business function—critics will not consider it art.

Key Tenet #4

The Fear of Loss is Highly Persuasive

An underappreciated concept among specialist and generalist dentists, when it comes to marketing for any type of dentistry, is how much patients are motivated by the fear of loss and how prevention of loss relates to most facets in each of our lives. This is the most powerful promotional message/tool for any product ("life without X is lousy"), service ("life without X would be unbearable"), political cause ("loss of X means Y to you"), or religious belief ("threat of loss of heaven/your own planet/virgin/angels dancing on pinheads").

Taking this into account, you would be foolish to not add "loss" components into every ad and promotional material in your practice; especially when the service you promote is good for people. Smile-Train, an organization that provides training and supplies to local doctors around the world in an effort to reduce the negative impact of cleft lips on children born in poverty with the condition, uses very graphic images of children with this condition in its advertising for donations. It vividly creates emotion and empathy for how this disfigurement will impact the child negatively. While this graphic loss oriented message offends some viewers (individuals who were already unlikely to donate), it leverages the power of loss to provide life changing benefits to the recipient of care.

Humans fundamentally don't like to give up something they have, whether it is tangible or intangible. The last financial panic that brought down several big banks on and off Wall Street is a powerful reminder of how fear of loss can create a financial panic among the masses. "Evidence-based" behavioral studies regarding everything from food, healthcare choices, and money repeatedly show that decisions are more swayed by losing, and the threat of such, than by a possible gain.

For marketing reconstructive or complex dental services, every contact with your target patients must focus on solutions for the specific problems they are plagued with and also on what happens when the problem is not solved (in terms of more loss).

The ultimate "fear of loss" motivator for any patient is missing teeth regardless of whether or not a patient is wearing dentures. A continual prodding and irritation about the deepest disability of all (toothlessness) and its consequences is a powerful motivator for all advanced services. If you had only one tool in your behavioral chest to help patients make better decisions, it should be this.

This "fear of toothlessness" motivator can cause patients with completely healthy dentition to show up for consultations after seeing an ad related to missing teeth or implants.

What about Gender and Motivation?

There are differences in what males and females fear to lose when it comes to their teeth.

Males "fear of loss" motivators

Loss of convenience
Speech impediments
Anything that reduces ability to date/have sex

Females "fear of loss" motivators

Looking old
Dull, worn teeth
Chipped teeth
Facial creases
Being seen without their dentures

It is important to include gender-specific motivators in promotional materials and to ask, via case-acceptance systems, for the specific motivators that resonate strongest with that individual patient. Including those gender-specific motivators as part of the case-presentation process helps to remind the patients what is important to them about their dental treatment.

Key Tenet #5

Mass Media Is Necessary for Finding Big Elective Cases

For a steady flow of patients who need reconstructive, implant, or other niche-oriented dentistry, two to three major forms of mass media (media that reaches many multiples of thousands of potential patients) are necessary to make enough of them aware of your practice that you can expect to do these procedures on a consistent basis. Why is that the case?

Reason 1

Most implant, full-mouth reconstructions, full-mouth periodontal services, denture wearers, and fearful patients are outside the normal dental practice and generalist-specialist referral systems. Other cases are in the wrong practice, being "cared" for by an ill-equipped colleague, and are not being offered solutions to their problems. Invariably, the provider will have issues: lack of case acceptance or training in Ethical Selling, selling services in a completely random fashion, a staff that does not believe in the doctor or the dentistry, clinical skills, fear of offering costly comprehensive options, or simply a fear of rejection.

Reason 2

Statistically, only 3–9.5 percent of "disaster" patients—those needing the most dentistry and searching for answers—will enter treatment in a given year (Private client surveys1996-Present). While finances are always a major factor, there are other readiness issues that prevent many from choosing "right now" as the time to pursue major treatment.

These dismal statistics are seldom discussed in the dental management, marketing, or consulting world because so few are aware of these percentages are as dismal as they are, willing to acknowledge them, or potentially able to propose workable answers. This statistic has held up in a variety of geographic locations (urban, rural, US, non-US).

In practical terms, 3–9.5 percent means that for a practitioner desiring to have twenty-four complex case patients enter treatment each year, 252–800 potential patients with the specific need must contact the practice and at least request information each year.

In some ways, the 3–9.5 percent is worse than Las Vegas slot machine odds. Slots return 85–95 percent of all bets! If the highly trained clinician enjoyed the same odds for patients needing significant care ultimately opting for it, out of those 252-800 prospects, more than two hundred cases would enter treatment in a year. This bottom-line percentage forces practices to be serious in how promotion is undertaken and how Ethical Selling must be attached to promotion.

The Need for Sales Systems and Qualifying Patients as a Consequence of Mass Media

Using two to three ongoing forms of mass media will generate enough interest in your advanced services to create a steady flow of the 3 percent to 9.5 percent who are ready for services. It will also create some interest from the 93–91.5 percent who are not ready, both in the short and long term.

This must be dealt with. Otherwise, the practice wastes time and becomes demoralized as it's simply to have numerous patients presenting to appointments who can only say no to services.

The importance and sophistication with how you qualify patients interacting with the practice—via requests for information, consultations, and case presentations—becomes critical in managing patients who aren't ready.

Without a system in place, you quickly reach a time limit in discussing potential treatments with those who inquire.

Additionally, over a period of years, the "not ready right now" patients can create another source of cases (another critical Academy Tenet is creating a Complex Case Annuity).

Never forget the ongoing role mass media plays in creating interest and cases. If you start believing that patients find your practice solely because of reputation or word of mouth, and mass media are eliminated "to save money," you quickly find that once the media are turned off, the cases fail to arrive.

Key Tenet #6

Three Types of Patients Respond to Elective Deep-Disability Marketing

In most Western countries, most forms of life-changing dentistry (implants, reconstructions, sedation, cosmetics) are private-pay services. Even in places where there is some state funding for major dental services (Norway comes to mind), reimbursement is never as simple as "signing up," sending the request for money, and waiting for the Wells Fargo truck to arrive. In environments where "free money" exists, there will always be patients who don't want treatment even though they have issues that would be solved by current procedures. A qualifying process unrelated to finances is still needed.

Outside of that rare instance where a "unicorn" of state reimbursement for major dentistry exists, remember that regardless of location and transient economic conditions, there are only three types of patients interacting with the business and entering your practice's Ethical Selling system via a first appointment. This is regardless of whether you market using ads, promote only to patients internally, or treat patients only on a referral basis.

Dr. John Kois, a highly respected clinical instructor, is known to say, "Teeth aren't for everyone. Some people can't have them. Some people shouldn't have them. Some don't deserve them." His observation comes close to landing on the fact that there are only three types of patients presenting to any practice.

Patient Type 1: The patient who will never have the financial means, or access to the means, for major treatment.

This is a reality for most patients with complex dental issues. Imagine the millions more who would have been cast into this position if water fluoridation has not arrived on the scene!

The reality of not having the means is not a moral or social justice or right or wrong. It is what it is: a reality.

One of the most inane questions in the profession is, "What are we going to do about these patients who don't have money?" Outside of your choice to perform a charitable case as you choose, nothing you, I, or "big brother" can do will change this fact of life. Step inside other businesses selling goods or services at similar price points, and no one is asking this question. The question becomes will you choose to focus on those who need, appreciate, and are capable and willing to purchase?

To keep patients who can only say "no" from mentally exhausting you, draining time, and inflating overhead, selling systems must automate the first steps that screen as much as possible. Doctors either embrace this or choose to get smart about this or they don't.

The solution is to give your prospective patients the tools to decide whether they are "in or out" and whether going on to diagnostics and treatment discussion makes sense for their situation. While denial can sometimes attach itself to hope (meaning that some Type #1 patients who are in denial even after traversing a well-designed screening system), the good news is that diagnostic fees and fee discussion strategies help the vast majority of these patients decide that complex case dentistry isn't for them without embarrassment to the patient or practice.

Patient Type 2: Those who say, "Doc, I don't have the money" yet forget the critical words "for you."

Patient Type 2 has the financial resources to devote to dental treatment. These patients usually have that amount and more, are already spending it on discretionary expenses, and choose to not invest it in themselves.

These patients might eventually go forward with treatment (emphasis on "might") if the dental or non-dental problem grows large enough in their mind that it outweighs the unwillingness to spent on themselves and they allow you to help them. Examples abound of those who have the means but for whom having a nice smile or functional health is not a priority.

Significant diagnostic fees are a screening tool that helps determine seriousness and financial commitment. Because these patients have the means to pay any fee and circumvent financial screening steps, you will find that some of them pay for diagnostics, go through your entire systematic approach to presenting the treatment options, consume your time, and still say no.

Beyond the presentation, they remain inside your follow-up system and are continually offered choices with the practice as time goes by.

Patient Type 3: The patient who can and will say yes.

About 35–70 percent of patients will say yes after interacting with well-designed marketing and systems for ethically selling services. They choose more optimum care, lifetime dentistry, quadrant care, full-mouth implants, and reconstructive dentistry.

They have the means (often having been diligent savers their entire life) or have access to the means (friends, family, or borrowing).

You see many variables with these patients in their manner of dress, general appearance, social history, where they live, and the cars they drive. There are so many people in this group who look like they could never afford the dentistry offered that no doctor or staff can guess who can and can't walk into the practice and write a large check (or, at times, pay with a stack of currency in a grocery bag).

Sadly, there are doctors who advocate checking the parking lot to see what cars patients are driving to decide whether or not they might invest in their health and well-being.

James Anecdote: It wasn't unusual that during departure from my office during the lunch hour, I'd run a quick mental "survey" of the types of vehicles patients were driving into the office. Whereas many dentists would be prone to see a nice car and think that surely the patient driving it would choose great options for their health, my experience was that those patients who needed serious dentistry and who presented in a more modest care were more likely to say yes. The fact that they weren't constantly investing in an expensive, depreciating asset (like a Mercedes or a "bad-ass" truck) was why they could make such choices.

Ultimately, life is like a roller coaster where some folks are on the fun side and going about their routines, which can include benefiting from major dentistry, in every economy, and others are on the side of the ride that is not as fun.

Key Tenet #7

Qualifying Steps, the Key to Finding Those More Likely to Say Yes to Treatment

When problem-solution messages related to niche, elective services (implants, reconstruction, cosmetics, sleep apnea treatment, TMD solutions, sedation dentistry, cosmetic dentures, soft tissue disease treatment, etc.) are put into the market through far-reaching mass media; significant numbers of patients inquire about the solutions offered. The greater the depth of the dental need (those patients with the most serious problems), the higher the interest and number of inquiries.

For the most dentally disabled patients (those needing full-mouth extractions or currently wearing dentures and seeking solutions), it's not unusual to generate six hundred to twelve hundred inquiries in a year by using mass media. Based on the long-term percentages followed in hundreds of practices, most of those who inquire will not be willing or financially able to say yes to significant treatment. The number of patients entering into treatment in reconstructive-focused practices is less than 9.5 percent of those who proceed with treatment in the year of the first inquiry when they have serious needs requiring more than $20,000 in treatment. Based on these percentages, of 1,200 inquiries, up to 1,140 of those inquiring are unlikely to enter treatment in the year of their first inquiry.

This presents a serious time-management issue for any practice focusing on complex procedures: which patients are more likely to opt for treatment and thus obtain the limited time available for consultations. "I spend too much time with patients who say no to my treatment options" is the most prevalent complaint among highly skilled clinicians making major financial investments in external promotion or in time commitments obtaining referrals because the end result is frustration with the numbers of cases moving forward.

This often leads to blaming ads and the referral process for not sending "the right patient," when in reality, the blame lies on the practice for not putting into place simple, predictable steps that allow patients to decide about the components of care (time, money, reasonable results, etc.). The patients should be able to decide if a next step is warranted *before* consuming valuable practice time. Blaming ads and continually seeking one "perfect" ad or ad venue diverts attention from the "qualifying hole" in the practice's way of selling dentistry. An additional result is that more patients are embarrassed and put into uncomfortable situations related to their financial standing. This reflects poorly on the practice at large and the individual dentist's level of professionalism.

Realizing that finding patients likely to choose significant treatment is equivalent to "searching for a needle in a haystack," the goal is to find better sorting steps that reduce time commitments for everyone (patients, staff, and doctor) and minimize embarrassment. In sales terminology, this is called "qualifying." Even nonprofit, charitable organizations qualify their customers.

Without qualifying systems, the practice faces statistics related to elective cases, involving significant investment from the patient, that are daunting. While statistics on the odds of success for elective cases are one thing of concern, at least two subjective aspects are underappreciated in the profession and almost never discussed from the meeting podium. One subjective, direct side effect of not creating qualifying stems is the negative impact on attitude and psyche related to constantly hearing "no" after major investments in developing predictable treatment options. The damaged attitude easily diminishes the confidence required for discussing major treatment, the general happiness in the workplace, and professional satisfaction. It even impacts development of treatment recommendations ("If they always say no, why bother recommending anything besides X?").

Rejection can be taken personally. Few in any business where a product or service is exchanged report that they enjoy investing hours of planning or conversation in a process that results in wasted effort and rejection. By social conditioning, few people like hearing no, even if it isn't about them personally. The majority of no's are related to patient readiness, financial circumstances and/or beliefs ("nothing personal, doc"), however, with enough occurrences, it can begin to feel personal!

Lack of an understanding about qualifying and failure to put appropriate steps into place related to such as a part of a system for Ethical Selling contributes to direct, ongoing discounting and devaluing of all dental services. Discounting is the path of least resistance ("I'll keep lowering the fee until someone says yes").

No provider has been "held at gunpoint" and told to reduce fees, yet the easiest solution, for those not selling via systems, hearing no routinely, is to continue to reduce fees to find a balance between the number of yeses and nos. Dentists falling into this thought pattern believe that every patient is motivated by cost and think, "I must discount to deal with this."

The consequence is reduced margins, and this can become an ongoing cycle and result in a downward spiral, threatening the business's ability to function. The businesses littering the "discounter's graveyard" are storied at

Wikipedia. Current examples, such as Sears, Kmart, and Best Buy, play out in almost real time the downward profit spiral related to ongoing discounting strategies.

Besides these subjective issues, one issue arising from too many no's (especially if they are made by the person in the chair) is objective. Needless no's waste immense amounts of time, a nonrenewable resource no matter one's age, location, number of years in practice, or clinical training.

A prominent motivational business speaker, Jim Rohn, was often quoted as saying, "You can always get more money, but you can't get more time." How much of this nonrenewable asset is committed to each prospective patient when moving from a phone call to a low-cost or "free" consultation, to diagnostics, case presentation, a question-and-answer follow-up visit, and additional phone calls with staff? Assuming that the practice has put into place a systematized selling system that provides the best odds of arriving at a yes to treatment, with all of the factors involved (financial, family, psychology of buying, etc.) taken into account, when all the time the doctor and team staff members expend interacting with the patient is added, it can easily total ten to fifteen hours per patient *before* the case goes into treatment. For the fearless, determine the salaries of the team (assistant, phone staff, office manager, doctor) and multiply that by the hours.

With the numbers on the table, a Harvard MBA is not required to understand that there's a limit to how many ten- to fifteen-hour increments can be expended without some yeses. If you have a systematic selling system, an acceptable acceptance range for complex cases (over $10,000) is 35—80 percent. If the yeses drop below 35 percent annually, a major issue in the sales or qualifying system must be investigated.

Ultimately, once you have a thorough understanding of the odds at work against you, the mental risks to your selling team, the objective time commitments and overhead, a realization is made that there has to be a simpler way. For practices committed to seeing these cases, that simpler way is the creation of and consistent use of "qualifying" steps for screening and for reducing the loss of time.

Automated Qualifying

The materials patients receive from the practice (information related to promotions and consultations) can help them qualify with minimal time investment. [These items are discussed at length in the Maximum Case-Acceptance Training Program for the ethical selling of dental services. Templates for developing your qualifying materials in your practice are provided. A trial in that Program is discussed at the end of this book.]

The "Funnel" Principle: Attaching Marketing to Qualifying, and More Reasons to Systematize

The connection between qualifying steps and marketing is often described as a "funnel," because it is easy to envision how the slopping sides of the funnel are created by patients moving through self-qualifying based on multiple factors (see figure 2).

An important reason to systematize the qualifying process as part of ongoing marketing strategies is to remove doctor and staff bias regarding which patients are likely to go into treatment (guessing who is qualified).

Think of the top of the funnel as the point where all prospective and existing patients enter the practice's case-acceptance (Ethical Selling) system (regardless of whether they were referred, acquired via external marketing, or were a long-term patient in a practice's dental hygiene system that decided it was time to discuss more comprehensive care).

The idea behind the funnel is to create a way for the patients who have the best chance at getting to "yes" to enter an effective yet time-intensive, case-acceptance system and remove doctor and team guesswork.

One of the most effective qualifying principles is including discussions related to fees and treatment time expectations early in the selling process. Include the time before the patient calls the office, when the patient visits the website, before the patient physically presents, before the patient's appointment from hygiene for a next step, and before diagnostic visits.

A simple, direct mechanism to create a qualifying step is to use a significant diagnostic fee, provided that you have communicated enough "reason why" messages related to the services offered (such as uniqueness).

Type 3 patients (willing and able to pay all diagnostic fees; discussed in Key Tenet 6) can still say no for nonfinancial reasons even when "money is no object" after moving past qualifying steps.

It's also important to realize that some patients, based on desire and motivations, choose to accelerate faster into the funnel.

If embarrassment and feelings of financial inadequacy are minimized as part of qualifying, and if effective long-term follow-up is a philosophy of continued Ethical Selling, a small percentage of patients, not initially qualified, can go into treatment years after their first interaction with the practice as their financial circumstances change.

Key Tenet #8

For Large Cases, Professional Dress and Teeth Is a Must;

As business has become far more serious after 2008, professional dress has returned to convey competency and authority in businesses that previously adopted a more relaxed dress code. Sound familiar? The same pattern emerged immediately following the dot-com bust at the turn of the century.

In past eras past, what you wore was *the* sign of wealth and social status, and the wealthy wouldn't be caught in public without a starched collar and three-piece suit. Times changed, starched collars went away, and many point out that today's super-wealthy are inclined to t-shirts, jeans, and flip flops. However, for every example of those multimillionaires, you'll find "Fortune 500 wealthiest" list members who dresses appropriate to their arena whether attending to business or personal matters.

Donald Trump is a good example. Try to find photos of him not wearing one of his uniforms of choice: a business suit or "just stepped off the golf course" attire. While most would prefer to always wear casual Callaway golf shirts (or cargo shorts/flip flops), when someone is asking another person for considerable sums of money, unless the product (or treatment plan) is being accepted on the eighteenth hole, the sport shirt isn't helping the case. To maintain high wages or elevate your ability as a high-wage earner, conveying competency and skill, and addressing as many trust-building factors as possible, are important, and casual attire is a detractor.

Many dentists are resistant to this notion. A fair number resent the dress code enforced on them in the university process. In the Seventies and early Eighties, smocks were common. The late Eighties and beyond saw the university dress codes switching to scrubs as a by-product of infection control. While infection control is important, allowing one's dress designed chair side cannot be allowed to negatively impact patient's perception of the value of your services or your competency in your services.

As the dress code shifted, full-mouth reconstructive dentistry became more predictable and widespread in the Nineties, courtesy of advanced institutes and training programs. Some astute observers in the profession began reporting their observations in online bulletin boards as case fee levels went up. The discovery was that patients opted for better treatment options when the doctor looked the part, which conveyed a message of "I know what I'm doing." While this was new to dentistry, high-wage earners in other industries responded, "Why did it take you so long to figure this out?" Too often, unless a thought originates inside the profession, it is not deemed valid or worthy of consideration.

Here's an excerpt from *Plain Talk about Leadership* by Robert L. Bailey, retired CEO of State Auto Insurance Companies and a frequent speaker on leadership.

Through the years I've been sold on the idea that if you are going to be a cowboy, you should dress like a cowboy. That means if you are going to be a doctor, you should dress like a doctor. (Periodically I see a doctor wearing blue jeans while making his rounds at the hospital, and if I were his patient, I would have somewhat less confidence in him.) If you are going to be a lawyer, dress like a lawyer. And if you are going to be a professional, dress like a professional.

As a professional observer of people for more than 40 years, I'm convinced that professionals tend to be less professional when they are dressed for washing the car. Some believe that the casual dress trend has had the effect of reducing the normal workweek by 20%. Some go so far as to try to avoid certain business transactions on casual Fridays because employees are more error prone. Furthermore, I find it offensive when my business transaction is being handled by a person wearing an 'I'm With Stupid or One's in the Oven' t-shirt. I just can't believe that my request for service is being given the care I expect. OK, so I lack a sense of humor.

Dress appropriate for your business—and dress the way you want your people to dress. (Plain Talk About Leadership, Robert L. Bailey, ISBN-10: 1931604010)

The best part of this phenomenon, and lack of understanding in the profession, is that it's easy to not do what everyone else is doing to use this tenet to your benefit.

Besides looking the part, common sales messages, often overtly or covertly said to patients, are "Enhance your career! Make more money!" For many high-level executives, salespeople, realtors, small business owners, and anyone who deals with the public, their mouth is how they make their money. Their communication, appearance, and self-confidence allow them to get their job done and help others. Could you imagine an entertainer or media person with unattractive teeth? Absolutely not! Their "look" is critical to their success.

There is science behind this statement. Attractive workers have been shown to be paid, on average, up to 14 percent more than unattractive workers, and it's true in the United States and Canada (Beauty and the Labor Market, Hamermesh and Biddle, The American Economic Review Vol 84 No 5)).

In the same vein of "beauty/good looks equals better results in many of life's endeavors," there's data on everything from political electability to lighter prison sentences based on nothing other than appearance

Some patients may state that the only reason they chose you over others is because you "look the part." While few would agree that this is a way to make a decision (that statement will infuriate many dental continuing education junkies who refuse to address non-clinical business issues), the best response is "thank you" and a great result.

Dentists can find custom-tailored attire for consultations and case presentation that will last a decade. Much like "custom smile design" under the eye of a skilled professional, a custom tailor can hide things that off-the-rack clothing can't. Even fifteen years ago, this type of service was available to only the wealthy. Thanks to outsourcing and the Internet, a traveling tailor can take your measurements and cut and sew a suit for the same price as a decent off-the-rack item from a department store.

Key Tenet #9

For Large Cases, Professional Teeth Are a Must

In the vein of "dressing professional" for the part, we arrive at your personal dental health and appearance.

If we tell patients they'll benefit financially and personally from functional dentistry that works well and improves their appearance, would not the same statement apply to the doctor? If you have unsightly teeth as the doctor, what does this suggest to your patient and customer about the faith you place in what you provide as a service?

When BMW began manufacturing several of their models in the U.S., one of the level employee benefits was leasing new vehicles to workers at very low costs because of the direct impact this had on the production workers believing in the goal of producing a quality vehicle with few defects. A pleasant smile is just as much a necessity for your team as they are a major of the in-person message you are send to patients about your belief in your services.

Teeth and dress impact cases, case size, and acceptance rates, but go to any major meeting (except for perhaps the American Academy of Cosmetic Dentistry) and count the great smiles on display. You will find more staff in good shape, in this respect, than doctors. This is akin to an implant-focused dentist exclaiming the virtues of dental

implants while he wears dentures and complains to everyone around him how poorly his eighteenth-century device
is working. Why would patients buy their dentistry (especially services paid for out of pocket) from a doctor whose
personal choices don't match the choice he or she is asking
patients to make?

Bonus: Being "Not Like the Rest"

A common thread running through many of the tenets of
the Academy relates to not doing things like others and in
fact it is an expression of the accumulated advantages discussed in the preface. In the doctor's smile, the staff appearance, the doctor's attire for case presentations, what's being
shown to the public to create phone calls, or in how Ethical
Selling takes place in the practice, the common thread is
positioning how what you do that is different from other
dentists. For the boldest, even calling out to patients who've
been to Chain ABC in promotional messages is a way to
insert yourself into the patients' thoughts about what they
didn't like in a consultation or treatment ("If you're unhappy
with your experience at ABC, here's why you should consider a visit or consult with…").

It's easy to create a list of "here's what you expect, have
probably experienced, and like at the dentist (with a list of
the things people hate)" and a list of "here's what you'll find
with us," setting the stage of "why we're different."

For Patients with More Serious Issues

A pathology instructor espoused, during a presentation,
that when viewing pathology slides, the first things to
consider are the most common entities (horses) versus the
ones that are one in a hundred thousand (zebras).

While that makes sense for diagnosing cancer and
for thinking about clinical conditions it's not what dental

patients with serious problems think about ("who can take care of this for me") when they are looking for help. The patients are looking for the "zebra"—not a regular dentist— even though in most markets, there are likely many facilities that could handle the same patient competently. Part of this positioning is addressing the conversation that the patient is having internally.

Why does anyone seek out the zebra? Everybody welcomes the convincing mystic, no matter what the product or service. People desperately want to believe that there is a long-lost, ancient, or revolutionary new cure or tonic, a formula for easy wealth with no work, happy relationships, better sex, well-behaved children, growing three-hundred-pound pumpkins, losing two hundred pounds, or a gizmo that turns dog feces into gasoline or tin cans into gold bars. They are looking for a "just tell me what to do" answer to believe in.

Patients want to believe that *you* have answers and techniques that others do not. They don't want rational explanations for what you do for them. They want to believe that you are the "zebra."

To position yourself as such, there are necessary items that make it difficult—or, on a practical level, impossible— to compare yourself to another. Competency at clinical dentistry is a vital, foundational piece of this puzzle but is only one component. Understanding this reality is step one. Looking for what creates that difference is step two, and step three involves the steps to get things done.

Key Tenet #10

Doctor and Staff Communicate to Reduce Complexity

Why must treatment discussions be simple? Studies about intelligence and wealth were previously covered as well as a discussion about average professional degree hold IQ. When it comes to face to face discussion with patients, via the doctor and team, it is important to remember that these principles apply not only in written form of written materials provided to patients and in direct advertisements to the public but also in personal communication between patients and you and your team.

It's likely that what two dentists conversing about during a clinical meeting would easily be understood between the two parties, Insert a patient into the same conversation, and most of the subject matter would be poorly understood. This is the situation most patients find themselves in when having discussions about treatment.

Fundamentally, if someone with a high school education can't understand what you're talking about doing for them as the provider, you are in trouble.

Your Competitor Is Helping You by Doing the Exact Opposite

The more complex something is, the more likely we are too simply 'tune it out' or, in situations where a decision needs to be made, find ways to not make or defer a decision. We'll call this the "rule of complexity." More complexity is bad for helping patients make good decisions.

Most dentists are routinely guilty of violating this rule regarding complexity. Dental technical jargon overwhelms the patient who out of confusion says no or simply never returns. This way of conveying information fits into the tried-and-true "educate the patient" philosophy (still the majority opinion in the profession), but leaves the dentist as constantly frustrated and wondering, "Why doesn't the world understand me?"

The next time a second opinion is seen in your practice, take great effort to simplify the discussions regarding treatment and watch "the light bulb go off" for the patient who finally has an understandable foundation from which they can base a decision.

"Yes" Doesn't Happen Nearly as Often without Understanding

The patient's world is complex enough. Daily life shows no sign of getting simpler. Technology has made things move faster and more efficiently but hasn't reduced the number of decisions being made. Behavioral science studies, such as those reviewed by Dr. Sheena Iyengar in her recent book, 'The Art of Choosing' shows that when something is complex, taking no decision is commonplace.

Decision-Making Energy Is Finite

Not only are decisions less likely to be made if a discussion is overly complex, but the more decisions made in a day means a person is less likely to take on risk as the day progresses. Stop doing case presentations in the afternoon and evening (or at least the ones you don't mind not going into treatment).

Case Acceptance Statistics and Time

Simple discussions mean that the most complex case can be presented in thirty minutes or less (not including financial discussions). Past the thirty-minute mark, case acceptance goes down as attention span dwindles and confusion about choices goes up. Nothing about this tenet means that your systems for Ethical Selling and marketing can be simplistic.

Dentistry is complex, and the marketing and selling systems for things that cost a lot of money (especially things that people don't crave or have a burning desire to purchase) are complex, but discussions with the purchaser should be kept simple. To eliminate complexity from your team's habits, record what's said in case presentations and financial presentations. No doubt someone on your staff has a smartphone that can make a digital recording. Get the presentation transcribed, and review it quarterly.

Key Tenet #11

Understand the Impact of the Phone on Bigger Elective Cases

When the question "besides the doctor's hands, and license to practice, what is the single most important thing in every practice?" is asked, answers range from the dental assistant, a hand piece or other cutting instrument, to the dental chair or sterilizer. Only a handful will correctly identify the item: the phone.

Members of the Academy are concerned about making the phone ring as well as the systems attached to the call, beginning when someone on the team takes a call or makes an outbound call. When the phone rings, it ultimately translates into patients being helped via the practice's services. Ultimately, answer calls correctly and using good phone systems puts revenue into the practice.

Eighty percent of new patients won't call back if they are calling to book an appointment and don't reach someone. Watch your personal behavior with voicemail when calling a business for the first time for more insight! New customers transferred to voicemail are more likely to return to Google's search menu where they will look for a practice with good patient reviews and try dialing again. Those two items alone should have any business owner seeking advantages that train their phone staff to eliminate this issue, yet only 25 percent of business owners feel that the phone is a very important to their business. There is a significant disconnect in belief about how important this device is by the business owner and in how it impacts their customers decisions. For dental practices, this disconnect translates into thousands of practices refusing to commit to ongoing training and measurement of this critical tool—which again provides one more of those advantages needed to deal with what is "unfair."

The phone provides a nearly universal guarantee of increased return on marketing and promotion activity, in any practice in any location. That increase in return is proven time and again in practices that regularly inspect their phone team and train them on an ongoing basis. Practices with ongoing training for phone teams and "sales drills" with the entire team are the highest performing, independent of economic conditions.

If the phone rings and inquiries are arriving about the practice's services, but case numbers are not growing, the hole in the system is a doctor or manager who doesn't know the importance of training related to the phone, friendly staff who mean well but don't have the right tools, or staff members who intentionally sabotage phone calls and don't want to take them or show any skill at communicating with the patient. While those are the real holes in the system, the ad or marketing usually receives the blame.

In situations where dozens of phone calls arrive and consultation appointments aren't being made, the front office members often state, "If the phone didn't ring so much, I could get my work done." A review of either a "mystery shopper phone call" recorded by the hired shopper (the outdated way) or of a live recording from a real patient phone call (the best method) would reveal the same staff members being often times pleasant, helpful, and acting as great information desk operators. Appointments would also be half-heartedly asked for, at best, and seldom secured on a routine basis. An "asking for the sale," which in many instances is a low-cost or free visit, rarely happens without training and knowing that it is a step in a phone system.

Dentistry attracts abundant nice, caring, well-meaning front office staff members who, without specific training, have difficulty giving away free appointments. With ongoing training, they secure even the most costly of prepaid diagnostic visits.

A few "old-timers" in the profession will tell you that there *was* a time, especially in implant dentistry, when the concept of no longer missing teeth or wearing dentures was so novel that patients would make treatment appointments on New Year's day if a doctor was marketing that new miracle. Those days are gone, and in today's environment, even with solution-oriented marketing generating phone calls every week, in a competitive market, you may get a single chance for the patient to schedule even a free appointment. In today's reality, no phone training means minimal results, no matter how well your marketing is generating calls.

As Alexander Bell's device is still the lifeline of any practice seeking advanced cases, it can't be ignored. How to handle the calls presenting to your practice, must be systematically trained. Return on investment (ROI) in marketing automatically goes up if the phone if part of your commitment to continual improvement.

Key Tenet #12

Use New Communication Technology to Your Advantage

Gone are the days when you could have three phone lines that rolled into each other and not think much past the "main line" being published. So many patients were calling that you could afford to lose 75 percent of the calls and still see year-to-year stability and growth in a practice.

In the past, practices weren't nearly as dependent on external marketing—many required none! The average patient coming in the front door bought dentistry as it was within the means of most middle-class individuals as a by-product of an insurance benefit (not completely eroded by inflation and more buying power). Many factors have converged to result in the current reality: fewer individuals choose dentistry in its one-tooth and more comprehensive forms.

As a sign of the fact that the "digging" is harder, it's now unusual if a practice doesn't have some form of external marketing at all times. Whether or not the marketing is especially effective is another conversation.

With all of the noise going on of practices trying to reach strangers and let them know what dentistry can do for them, the costs for reaching the potential patient, much less acquiring a patient, have dramatically increased. It's expensive to talk to strangers. It's even more costly to reach out to talk to strangers who have specific problems (missing teeth, battered teeth, fear, need specialized services, etc.).

As costs have increased, addressing critical points where case acceptance (e.g., selling) is being wrecked needs attention, or more money and cases go "poof!" These points in case acceptance or the selling process that get blown up can be thought of as "Points of Poof" or POP. One such POP, without a doubt, is when phone calls arrive. Those who train and inspect for POP get the best return from marketing expenditures, and those owners tend to expect a lot more from the people being given good phone tools.

A lot of technology has come along that can greatly improve results and reduce POP. Be aware of those technologies and use those you feel can help the most considering your practice specifics.

Here's a list of phone-related technology and team activities that make real differences in your results and minimizes phone POP.

Calls from external marketing (expensive phone calls) ring on a designated phone line.

Incoming calls from marketing are acknowledged as very important by doctor and staff which changes the mindset of the value of all calls.

Staff incentives are used related to calls arriving via marketing.

Call forwarding to cellphones is in place when external marketing is bought.

Live calls are recorded and the appropriate team members are trained weekly (daily, for the truly ambitious) for improvement.

Academy-provided online marketing phone tools are used to analyze call volume for calculating ROI on individual marketing strategies and ads and for final cost per new patient from marketing.

Your team attends a monthly dedicated phone training program.

Offices with a small staff use a phone attendant service to prevent calls from going to voicemail during regular hours and when external marketing is active.

Super advanced: A trained phone attendant service is used 24/7.

If appropriate, recordings of first-interest patient calls are reviewed with the team before consulting with the new patient.

Key Tenet #13

Understand the Concept of Real-World Readiness

Your practice and team invest time, financial resources, and energy to create interest and inquiries, by external or internal promotion, from prospective patients about your complex services. Out of everyone expressing interest, some prospective patients are ready for services, but most are not because of the following:

- Finances

- Fear

- Reality of young (and not so young) children and financial commitments therein

- Work or social time constraints

- Don't feel their problem is large enough

- Both spouses have the same clinical problems

- They're just looking into it (research phase)

- Insert reason here: _____.

Articles aimed at the profession often state, "Every patient has the ability to choose comprehensive care." While it makes for exciting reading, back in the real world, this statement isn't true. Just as it's impossible for every patient to always opt for their best health even when they desire to do so, it's impossible for the practice to have 100% of patients (even when finances are not a concern) saying yes to treatment. Based on member surveys, 35-70% is a common acceptance "rate" when cases sizes go beyond $10,000 in treatment and when treatment is proposed while following the Academy taught ethical selling system.

Key Tenet #14

Use Systems to Shorten Patient Buying and Decision-Making Time

Patients with complex problems had those problems develop but over a period of years. It is simpler for most patients with serious issues to continue putting treatment off versus dealing with it. It's human nature. Ultimately, this can result in the condition growing worse and requiring a more complicated and costly solution. Shortening the decision-making time is in everyone's best interest.

Realties of the Patient with Serious Dental Conditions

Here are some truths about patients with complex dental problems. It's important to realize their journey. Acknowledging where they've been is a component of creating trust.

For some patients, their situation evolved under direct dental supervision. The occlusion deteriorated, periodontal issues advanced, or more teeth were lost because of failures in clinical knowledge or practice systems, be they clinical, administrative, or sales oriented. In most cases, the patient with serious problems exited the preventive dental system due to financial reasons at the time or traumatic experiences. Others grew up mostly or completely outside the preventive system, leaving them with multiple strikes against them and a lifetime of minimal dental needs. For these groups, the result is frequently someone who has been away from dental technology and solutions for a decade or more. Their dentition has already tipped past the point of predictable return to health, especially when viewing the patient from a lifetime risk assessment (KoisCenter.com).

Not counting those who also got unlucky in the genetic dental dice roll, there are millions who could have stayed healthy if they had been inside the preventive system. That system is the one most in the profession are familiar with and fundamentally understand—it's the main item discussed in the educational system and the one that evolved around the insurance schemes from outside the profession and referral schemes inside the profession. The vast majority of dentists are familiar with this situation.

Regardless of the numbers of patients living around every practice, average practitioners have a hard time believing they exist even when confronted with photos of typical dentition. They see the world from inside the system that they are used to: patients with only a few problems needing to be addressed.

Those promoting their services to these deep-disability patients understand that they are everywhere and that there are different rules, and a much different approach, to reach them and ethically sell to them. This issue of protracted decision-making time is one more piece of that puzzle.

Stasis is the Norm for the Complex-Case Patient

A psychological consequence of a problem developing over an extended period, versus an acute issue, is that the built-in resistance to treatment. The pattern of delay and doing nothing is well established. Patients say, "Why address something that barely bothers me and doesn't seem to be that much worse today than yesterday? After all, it's not going to kill me, right?"

Buying Decisions Are Easily Prolonged by Additional Factors

Other factors work in favor of preventing a decision: responding to your marketing, showing up for appointments, and saying yes, financially and non-financially.

For the complex patient, entering treatment has immense benefits, but the astute observer understands that humans are driven more by the fear of losing something than by the possibility of gain. The fear of pain, cost, the inconvenience of treatment, the age of children (both young and adult), the length of time of treatment, work or social time constraints, not feeling that the problem is significant enough, or just starting their research—all these play into compounding and reinforcing the state of doing nothing.

As clinical symptoms come and go, and social and daily functional issues grow and then recede, the likelihood of deciding can wax and wane. Is it any wonder that most of the profession is stymied by what is happening on the patient's side of this equation while the dentist is ready to serve and offer an answer?

A key understanding related to these patients, in regard to marketing to them or the sales process, is realizing that the first time the "hand goes up" isn't necessarily when the patient is ready to enter treatment. In all your interactions, provide a compelling reason that "right now" is the time to choose treatment in terms of benefit and loss, emphasizing loss. If ignored, you miss real opportunities to disrupt the patient's pattern of putting things off and the situation becoming worse.

Encouraging a "right now" state of mind is an important part of dealing with human nature. By our nature, we all manage and arrange life's needs in a ranking fashion according to what is more pressing. You and your patients will delay decisions if whatever is being considered becomes a lower priority as compared to something new development. Always keep in mind to:

- Present treatment with losses amplified whenever possible.

- Make sure questions are answered related to treatment being considered ("shock and awe" packets help remove unknowns for the patient while emphasizing what patients gain and lose if they delay treatment).

- Approach follow-up differently compared to typical practices. Because patient readiness comes and goes, the practice that stays in contact with patients ultimately has more of these patients choosing that practice for treatment, and it has higher returns on the marketing investments made to find these patients.

- Make extra efforts to create "overwhelming evidence" with compelling reasons that you are the doctor to handle certain clinical conditions based on training and experience.

Recognize that decision-making time is more complex than previously believed. Practices can add components into their promotion and Ethical Selling systems to combat the innate tendency for complex-case patients to do nothing and help them get back to dental function and comfort.

Key Tenet #15

To Reach Those Who Aren't Ready "Right Now," Use Follow-Up Systems

This is the typical pattern for most practices:

1) Place dental advertising.

2) Get phone calls.

3) Schedule patients from the calls.

4) Ignore the patients who called but didn't make an appointment.

5) Go back to step one.

The problem with this pattern is that step 1, while a necessary part of doing business, is costly, and it's folly to not want to maximize every bit of the investment. Step 4, when not understood and left unaddressed, even over two to three years, results in lost opportunities with dozens of patients who could have been helped if the practice had kept in touch.

The more complex the case the practice seeks, the more important step four becomes to prevent waste in how you approach finding patients interested in complex services from a long term perspective. The cost to generate a single phone call related to a complex procedure can cost more than $100 per call and more than $1,000 per case started. Taking those numbers into account how could one not be interested in helping more of patients that a typical practice ignores?

Addressing this is as simple as instituting the use of a phone slip and an Excel database separate from the patient-management software. The patients who call are known to have a specific problem, and given enough time, some of these patients become ready for services because of changes in their circumstances.

The additional investment in maintaining contact is a tiny percent of the original cost to generate the phone call, yet without this minimal maintenance investment, the patient will quickly forget that you exist.

Few practices put in the minimal effort to set up a system of follow-up, even though the benefits are no secret. Will you be one of those who rise to the challenge to commit to simple, long-term follow-up for patients with serious problems?

.

Key Tenet #16

Follow-Up Never Ends

Patients with complex problems have had those problems develop over many years. They enter and exit states of being ready for treatment due to multiple factors at play in their lives. Some of those factors are related to dentition, but most are not. Every patient is on a roller coaster ride called life, and it's impossible to guess whether a patient is on the "fun" part, the dull part, the too-distracted part, or any part where everyday life gets in the way of needs, big and small, including getting dentistry. Few dentists understand the importance of this, falsely believing that their "universe" is more important than those of most patients and potential patients. Understanding these facts is important, because these realities impact thinking and specific actions related to marketing and case acceptance.

Success with large cases and at fee levels beyond insurance maximums depend on systems that make the rules work in your favor for patients deciding to do something good for themselves and for keeping them motivated to move forward. Few in the profession will acknowledge these realities or make efforts where needed—that's great news for those who do.

Practice case acceptance/selling statistics show that in a given year, only 3–7 percent of complex-case patients inquiring about advanced services will pursue treatment during that year when the total treatment plan is $10,000 or higher. This percentage is such that only the transaction size makes the marketing cost feasible from the perspective of the amount of time and percent of revenue spent letting these prospective patients know the services exist. The 3–7 percent constitutes what you could euphemistically call "low-hanging fruit." These patients call, are ready within a few months, and go forward with treatment. Most practices focus only on the low-hanging fruit because that's the way it has always been done in a professional practice. The practitioner thinks, "If you don't come in right now, I'll move on to someone else."

You can pick only "low-hanging fruit," but such a limited strategy is pure foolishness when you realize how much is being invested to create interest for a complex case. It does not make financial sense to "throw away" potential patients who contact the practice and aren't right in the short term. It is financially prudent to expend effort getting some of the "higher up fruit" (the 94–97 percent) to eventually become low enough to "pick" through follow-up. "Higher up" fruit was paid for, in most cases, years ago by some form of expensive marketing. Eventually the patients become ready because a small, ongoing investment was made to stay in touch with people who inquired about complex services but weren't ready in the short term.

For some practices, this lack of follow-up is the difference between success and failure. With enough yeses from complex-case patients entering treatment, this makes the ROI high enough to warrant the ongoing efforts to attract them.

As time passes, some patients in the 94–97 percent will enter treatment if they continue to hear from your practice. If they don't hear from you, they will forget every good effort you made to let them know about what dentistry can do. In their next search, they will find someone else.

Here are examples of follow-up steps that need to be included in your administrative and selling systems.

Ultra-Short-Term Follow-Up to Phone Calls, Web Requests for Information, after Free or Low-Cost Consultations

In the ultra-short term, follow-up is as simple as this:

1) A phone call ensuring that requested information was received.

2) The staff writes a note card, welcoming the patient after the initial introduction to the practice (free or low-cost consultation).

3) A phone call to book the next step (diagnostics) if the answer wasn't definitive at the live appointment.

Slightly Longer Short-Term Follow-Up (Diagnostics, Presentation, and within a Few Months after Presentation)

For patients who have gone through a diagnostic and presentation process, follow up includes the following:

1) Short note, written by the doctor, letting them know that you're still thinking about them.

2) Question-and-answer appointments following the treatment/financial presentation.

3) Additional phone calls related to financing or calls to keep the case moving forward, especially if a

yes was obtained but treatment won't start for an extended period.

4) Follow-up letters at specified intervals following case presentation to further motivate based on fear of loss or areas of gain that mean something to that patient,

5) Additional loss motivators when the agreed-upon treatment fee will no longer be valid (e.g., fee expiration).

Long-Term Follow-Up (Post diagnostics and Those Who "Raised Their Hand" Over the Years)

Long-term follow-up is where you win more of the "higher-up" fruit that is becoming ready for treatment. Think of a business you interacted with that kept in touch with you for the long term. How many can you name? One or two – if even that.

This is a big secret that few in the profession understand. Long-term follow-up stimulates your regular patients and large-case patients. Think of those responding to marketing over many years as your private, prospective case "holding tank." To keep them interested and aware for the long term requires throwing them something that reminds them of the practice on a regular basis. After years of marketing for the cases you enjoy the most in your practice, you build a "big case" annuity to pull from. This reduces the amount of ongoing external marketing needed and becomes a tangible asset that can be sold with the practice, sold on its own, or kept to build a new big case-only practice.

For the Long Term

As the number of e-mail received overwhelm the recipient, the advantages of offline communication returns. Use offline newsletters, periodic "how are you" postcards, and postcards related to end-of-year issues (insurance benefits, fees, fee increases). E-mail, e-mail newsletters, and video e-mail are OK, but remember that these methods are the easiest to ignore or delete.

Another effective method for long-term follow-up is to incorporate news into your message. An example of a news-related promotion could be offering your own "stimulus package" leveraging off the news about a governmental stimulus. A number of Academy members used that concept to book an entire summer's worth of business. One promotional piece ran through a test practice, celebrating the fortieth anniversary of the lunar landing with a $1,000 gift card applicable to cases $10,000 or more. It generated eleven phone calls, all from long-term prospects in the "holding tank" and now interested again, and led to three advance-paid $700 consultations, booked within two weeks, and one $15,000 case. These are perfect examples of cases that were paid for by previous marketing.

Everyone needs a reason to do something or take action, and news is one of the easiest ways to create a reason for your services.

When Does Follow-Up End?

The answer is easy: when the patient buys, dies moves away, or says, "Take me off your list."

For the Short Term and Long Term

None of the items discussed above are complicated, and they do not need to be complicated. They need to be ongoing. Marketing is a repetitive process just like the maintenance of prosthetics and dentition. As part of that repetitive process, weekly and monthly reviews of case-acceptance tracking should be part of your systems.

An annual marketing calendar reviewed weekly with doctor oversight/direction, doctor/manager discussions allows the practice to stay on top of tasks related to promotional efforts. Staff or vendor delegation of "to do" items that turn deadlines into actions are the best ways to keep marketing and follow-up on track.

Those who follow up for the long term have far more cases and far greater results from the same investment in marketing. This concept is so important that here's an example from the real world.

Everyone wants patients to buy immediately when they contact the practice. The reality is that some are ready right away (a small percentage), some will be ready in the months and years ahead (another small percentage), and some will never be ready (the majority.)

Understanding that there is a short-term and long-term sales cycle to everything, including significant dental services, is important for setting up the details for improving case acceptance/Ethical Selling results as well as keeping a clear mind on why certain actions are important.

The short-term sales process is well documented via the Ethical Selling Program taught to Academy members for new inquiries as well as those who come in for diagnostics and case presentation. As there are patients who contact the practice but do not immediately come for consultations, it's worth to talk further about long-term follow-up. This is called "Keeping In Touch" or KIT.

Too often, doctors get too caught up in dreaming up complicated, long-term follow-up steps that create road blocks to long-term, predictable follow-up. Make it complex and difficult, and most certainly it won't get delegated and done!

Some specific annual items need to be on the yearly agenda or what to send to regular patients and potential complex-case patients specifically related to the calendar turning. Outside of that, postcards and newsletters are more than adequate for creating more cases out of the prospective patient who have contacted your practice over the years.

What about e-mail? While automatic e-mail responders are not a bad idea, the reality is that after the first few months of emails, more often than not the DELETE key comes into play, which forces offline follow-up steps.

Recently, one of the Elite alumni, from a busy Chicago area practice, sent this note to one of our staff members that helps explain the economic rationale of what is at stake.

Dear Members,

I hope everyone is having a great summer. Just wanted to share with everyone how one should never underestimate the power of keeping in touch/contact with your prospective patients. I send a newsletter (Done for Your Practice out to my Big Case Database every two months. The last newsletter we sent brought us over 60K in production just this week. I closed a 50K implant case on someone that requested info 8 months ago and a 12K crown and bridge case on the wife of another person that requested info three months ago.

This is a reminder that these ongoing follow-up stems are too important to let fall through the cracks. These same patients will simply forget about you or forget about what you can do for them.

I am attaching and sharing my newsletter to hear some feedback.

This result described was due to a follow-up newsletter that in all likelihood required less than one dollar to mail to the patient. Here's my follow-up response to the doctor which was also sent to our Academy members.

Irfan,

Thanks for reinforcing the power of KIT (aka keeping in touch). As I hate to sound like a broken record on the subject, you will see me push on this three or four times a year.

Now that summer is in full swing and fall is already on the horizon, for the alumni, this is also a reminder to think about the sequence of pushing on prospects in the fall related to fees and insurance. Remember that the annual cycle of business activity waxes and wanes and can be altered based on the "noise" made to prospects and patients.

Back to the additional $60K in production. Even if ultimately several thousand dollars of offline "done for your practice" newsletters were sent, the return in treatment is significant. Those prospective patients cost $$ to acquire and the ongoing contact, while still an investment in marketing, brings a higher return because the "KIT" is less costly than acquiring.

If you weren't making sure that the practice was using a follow-up system, it is likely that the treatment would not have been done at all OR it would have been done by someone else. To the folks sitting on a prospective patient list, the more times they hear from you, the more they see you as their dentist/ surgeon, even if they haven't met you!

These are why offline follow-up (newsletters, postcards, and letters) works:

Think about the age ranges for those who like things printed.

Offline newsletters, to the uninitiated, sound like some-thing passé or last century, but they are still one way to gener-ate cases from your prospect list as time marches by, especially with those over the age of fifty. Things that can be felt, touched, or taped to the fridge are more powerful.

Anytime I jokingly mention that we might move the Academy's member letter to online only, the feedback is negative, not that I have ever had any serious intention of such. People like a physical product in their hand, and that product hangs around much longer than the 0s and 1s that constitute digital things. Many reach an email overload "tipping point." E-mail in-box clutter has reached a tipping point for many consumers. Think about when you open your e-mail reader or log in to your e-mail account(s). Do you dread doing it because of the volume of e-mail you expect to see? That's being repeated millions of times across the age spectrum. The most time-conscious grownups, aware of time wasted and mortality, see the "time vampire" at work and institute schemes to break free of the time drain. They hit the DELETE key faster, and some declare "email bankruptcy" (Google it).

These are the "worse than Vegas odds" even with the world's best Ethical Selling "case-acceptance" system. Only 3–9.5 percent of those patients (deep-disability cases) contacting the practice will opt for treatment above $10,000, but several more opt for treatment in future months and years if you stay in touch with them.

What are the long sales cycles and sales process for expensive things? When you see beat up dentition, how many years did it take for that to happen? How long did it take for the patient to finally decide to investigate a solution? If there's no problem-solution marketing used in their location, it might never even happen!

Without bumping into the right people in dentistry, you could go an entire career never hearing that sales cycles take longer for things that cost a lot of money, including all the great stuff technology, procedures, and materials in dentistry can do. It's reality.

The majority of dental offices, even those looking for comprehensive cases, don't follow-up beyond one or two phone calls. If the sale isn't made right then, they move on. Tie the lack of seriousness about putting a sales process into place, along with ignorance of variations in sales cycle lengths, and you see why most never break the "da Vinci code" of repeatable, comprehensive cases. It's what kept me from doing so for the first six years of my practice!

Great going Irfan.

Viva la follow-up!

James

Key Tenet #17

Proclaim Yourself the "Wizard" and Create a Category of One

Continue Education, Credentials, and Patients

There's a problem with credentials of any kind and piling up massive amounts of CE credits. Patients don't understand any of it. It's a basic assumption that you are "keeping up" like every other dentist. The smell in your office, the gouges on the walls, and stains on the carpet will cause far more cause for alarm than whether or not you attended a weekend CE course or a twenty-weekend continuum with live human surgery. To the patient, all that is the same, and all the titles of courses and the letters after your name are gibberish. A fair number of dentists don't even understand that letters such as PC or LLC are not academic titles!

The harsh reality is that you can have more CE credits than 90 percent of the dentists around you, and patients will be just as likely to pick someone with no credentials unless you take some specific actions. As dentists, we might pick our coursework based on reputation or the five-inch-thick CV of a presenter, but patients do not make decisions that way. If you help them understand what these things mean in ways that matter to them, and that they find important, in their language, it will directly contribute to patients picking you and to more cases going forward.

The Academy's trademarked Maximum Case Acceptance System spends time on how to incorporate the right discussions about continuing education and credentials into the "shock and awe" packets developed for the practice and for specific niche services being provided by the practice.

Why One of a Kind? Why Expert Status?

For the highly trained doctor, putting together a specific combination of training, credentials, and techniques so that you are "one of a kind" in your local market is one of the best ways to fight the "all dentists are the same" problem that exists in every competitive marketplace. We are all the same in the patients' eyes.

Being seen as the expert is a direct side effect of building your one-of-a-kind status in procedures, facility, methods, training, and staff and understanding that deliberate promoting such status is necessary to make your practice a "go to" reality.

A critical distinction is that declaring yourself an "expert" is not the same as saying "I'm the best," a phrase that most boards frown upon and that doesn't resonate well with patients. You can declare "I'm the most recognized expert in ABC-ville" without stating "I'm the best." The patient will infer it.

In the same vein, most boards prohibit the word "painless," even though the right methods make dentistry just that. This is a hundred-year holdover from days gone by and not because current scientific evidence shows that dentistry cannot be painless. For this scenario, having others (third parties) declare that services provided by you as a dentist have been found by them to be painless is perfectly acceptable because you are not the one proclaiming it.

THE DENTIST'S UNFAIR ADVANTAGE   ◆   DR. JAMES R. MCANALLY

How to Build Your Unique Status

Here are a few items that automatically help put you in the "category of one" especially when attached to your work flow (your method) of dentistry which could include:

- Immediate loading implants

- Conscious or intravenous sedation

- Risk-assessment profiles (as taught at the Kois Center)

- DNA periodontal disease susceptibility testing

- Speed of treatment based on either lab availability or technology

- Dental promises or warranties outlining what happens after services are performed,

- Performing all treatment in one office or having a unique umbrella via specialists or generalists all well versed ethical selling

Competition and being commoditized are ongoing realities for every business. Here are more reasons for becoming the wizard in your practice location:

1) It makes more of your competition irrelevant. It's true that you are competing mostly against (insert any number of consumer goods and services here). However, out of the patients who are purchasing dental services, some of them will consider competitors simultaneously, so why not eliminate as much of that as possible?

2) It makes it harder to cost compare. "Apples to apples" comparison means commodity pricing, a situation that many retailers are trapped in. It is difficult to compare different categories of products or services (apples to oranges). Dentists have the

ability to choose to package their services in bundles that reduce cost comparison since the service is no longer the exact same thing.

3) It allows fees appropriate to the skill level and for the factors required to be the "category of one" and to deliver something unique. For most, this means fees which are higher than competitors.

Be One of a Kind—Forever!

As time passes and technology, materials, and techniques come and go, another aspect of this concept of "being a wizard" is that part of your evaluation of whatever is new and at your disposal as the clinician is to ask, "How does this keep me in the category of one?" Make sure that anything new is discussed with patients in ways that mean something to them, not just to you or your team.

Who Will Declare You the Wizard?

You need to have credentials and a package of services and methods that make you unique. That's a given. You have all those things, now what? Who is going to say, "Dr. Veitz, you are the expert here in Dusseldorf"?

For the answer, take a look in the mirror. It's up to you to declare your expert status via your promotional materials and marketing. It is up to you to show that message to your patients and potential patients at every possible chance. If you happen to be at or near the pinnacle of the profession on a national or international level with dentists flocking to your clinical presentations, you will be declared an expert as a by-product of this attention from peers. This declaration by peers is unlikely for those not in the national or international spotlight.

THE DENTIST'S UNFAIR ADVANTAGE   ◆   DR. JAMES R. MCANALLY

If you wait for your local colleagues to make this declaration, you'll wait your entire life. If you get lucky and your local dentists declare it after a few decades of meetings and table clinics, you'll have thrown away most of your peak years of practice. Don't chance it. Develop the story and declare it yourself. Be the wizard.

Key Tenet #18

Your Staff Must Believe in You as the Expert and Wizard

We're in an economic age in dentistry where wasting any resource (time, human, capital) is no longer an option. The concept of eliminating waste includes missed opportunities related to persuading and influencing behavior and reinforcing why it's great for prospective patients to consider treatment and the services that can greatly improve their quality of life.

Ultimately, your team plays an important role in reinforcing why patients can trust and count on your clinical skills. Part of this conveyance of trust via on your team's interactions results in patients being thrilled to have found you and your team. It also results in expressions that the fee for the dentistry is worth its price.

Your staff has to believe in you as the expert in order to come across as sincere and communicate this belief to existing patients and prospective patients coming to consultations. These conversations, occurring regularly and automatically, boost case acceptance. When they aren't occurring or the wrong conversations are routine, case acceptance drops automatically.

The "staff as missionary" for your services is greatly under-appreciated. You have to be legitimate in your education, credentials, and behavior. In other words, to get your staff to "sell your story," you must "walk your talk" to your patients and staff.

For your team members to understand how they can help in this regard, it must be brought to their attention in team meetings. Let them know that patients instinctively look to the staff for guidance on what to expect, for insight on how they will be treated, what the experience will be like, and even whether they can trust the doctor. Without bringing this to their attention, it's unlikely they will understand the influence they have over patient decision making.

Their impact on patients extends beyond the consultation aspect of care and into the treatment phase. It includes reinforcing the patients' judgment that they made the right decision to spend substantial sums on their dental health, preventing and reducing "buyer's remorse," and it an impact on how happy a patient is when your work is finished. Most practitioners can relate to the experience when a treatment rendered was near perfect but the patient wasn't pleased at the end of the treatment. Invariably, reinforcement conversations did not happen during active treatment to help manage patient expectations.

Here are some key points to make in these discussions.

"You've made the right decision. Dr. Jones is the best in the field. She's *the* expert when it comes to your situation. If I had this kind of problem, she is who I'd want to see."

"We'll take good care of you just like the patients whose photos you see on our walls. I'm sure you'll be happy with your result, just like they were."

"Yes, this kind of dentistry is expensive. I can't count the number of times patients in your same situation said they wished they hadn't waited so long to get their dentistry done and were glad they spent the money."

"Dr. Jones is the best. It's difficult to find real experts these days. You're lucky you found her."

"You're lucky. Dr. Jones doesn't agree to take on every patient, only the ones that she knows she can really help."

"I know this may be hard to believe after all the years of problems with your teeth, but you really have found the right place and doctor for your situation."

Where there are multiple doctors (partnership) or associates, they can say things about you and your skills that you can't.

"I can tell you that among all the dentists I know in Townville, Dr. Jones is absolutely the one you need to see."

"If you haven't noticed by now, Dr. Jones is even recommended by more of her fellow dentists than other's in the region. She's going to take great care of you."

Much of the power of this tenet, from 1990-2008, was related to case acceptance on extremely large cases. In the post-2008 reality, it is a *must* at every fee level.

In the industrialized West, any business that duplicates services of multiple competitors is battling for a shrinking, middle-class customer base that can buy nonessential goods and services (dentistry being a nonessential service). Dentists battle this trend in their practices. To avoid discounting and sacrificing margins requires constant reinforcement of the practice and the doctor's status as the expert externally (via marketing) and internally (via marketing and staff conversations).

What is said or how it is said, by phone, e-mail, or in person, requires coaching, reinforcement, and monitoring on a continual basis. Team members must be expected to interact with patients correctly in these matters. The administrator or doctor must be aware that inappropriate conversations occurring via team members with inadequate skills can easily drive away new or existing business. With training, coaching, feedback, and measurement available, such actions cannot be tolerated under the new economic rules.

How to Coach, Give Feedback, and Reinforce

The easiest way to remind your team of the importance of having these sales-influencing conversations on the phone and in the practice is in your morning team huddle and weekly team meetings. This is an ongoing activity.

How to Monitor

Phone monitoring is done by pulling a phone call from a phone system that captures and records live patient phone calls for weekly review. Whether your 'phone team' consists of one staff member or more, if there is a desire to review additional calls, encourage it!

In-office conversation monitoring is done by the office manager and doctor listening for conversations between staff and patients. Reinforcement when your team members say the right things with a "good job" and "way to go" is as important as catching them doing the wrong thing.

Don't underappreciate the fact that it's human nature to sense when someone doesn't believe in what they are selling or discussing. In 'Thinking, Fast, and Slow' Dr. Daniel Kahneman discusses several studies showing that our hardwired instincts can detect incongruence that translates to avoidance behavior within milliseconds. This instinct happens so fast that the only way to prevent natural avoidance behavior is to eliminate the underlying incongruence.

If an individual on your team doesn't believe one hundred percent in the doctor, team, and value of the services for providing patients with beautiful smiles, comfortable teeth, and a better quality of life (for themselves, their spouse, significant others, their kids, grandkids, virtually everyone the patient comes into contact with), this team member damages your practice and your patients' decision making.

Key Tenet #19

Use Staff Time (Group or Individual) to Focus on Prospective Cases; Otherwise, the Ceiling of Complexity Damages Success

It took several years of monitoring dozens of practices to realize that it was simply not possible to attain a certain level of success in dentistry without staff meetings.

When questioned what his monthly staffs meeting routines were, one doctor's reply was, "I have a regular staff meeting—once per year!"

A weekly staff meeting is one of the first items that a basic management consultant will implement in a practice. For dentists new to team meetings, most will feel that there is no way they can give up one or two hours of production time each week "just to talk."

It's common that in even a modestly growing practice, a year after instituting a weekly team meeting, production doubles. Famed management guru, Peter Drucker, discovered something more than a half a century ago in the workplace that still stands true: Anything measured improves. This is what happens in practices as monthly statistics are monitored related to production, downtime, and hygiene.

Ongoing staff meetings are a "must do" and are recommended for every practice affiliated with the Academy. There are practices that must be "broken in" to begin having ongoing staff meetings. Most dental teams that violate this principle are controlled by doctors with under-developed leadership skills who are often afraid of confrontation with staff. The good news is that leaders are developed, not born!

The rule of needing an administrative "check in" applies no matter how many hours of clinical practice occur in a week. An oversight meeting with the owner or manager still matters. As an extreme example, even a one-day-per-week clinical practice will need a once weekly forty-five minute meeting with the manager the day before patients are seen.

Beyond the team meeting as a basic "measure, discuss, and improve" concept, another reason for having staff meetings, even in mundane practices, is that regardless of how simple the procedure mix, team members need to constantly be reminded how important their role is in the success of the practice.

As the complexity of procedures grows, so does the complexity of operations of employees. This is even truer in a business where marketing/sales, production, and operations are all under the same roof and team members have their hands in multiple departments. If there are two layers of management (doctor plus office manager, complexity increases further. It takes regular meetings and basic systems reviews to keep the ship sailing smoothly *and* growing. In larger businesses, you find a staff meeting just for operations, one just for sales, and another just for marketing, and middle managers working to smooth issues between competing areas and factions.

Procedures, Ceilings of Complexity, and Team Meeting Interplay

The business of dentistry has an innate level of complexity that builds based on types of procedures performed, location/competition, the number, quality, and tenure experience of the staff, and the personality and leadership ability of the dentist and office manager. A ceiling of complexity is always looming, limiting what is possible without the right systems, staff, mindset, and training and ongoing reinforcements with the team. When the ceiling is reached, new systems must be adopted to push it higher and grow into the new space.

When a practice adds in more cases requiring complex services like implants, reconstructions, or whole-mouth treatment via sedation, a new ceiling of complexity is formed.

For most practices, especially those outside structured Programs designed for addressing this issue, performing those services (not the clinical part but the business part) isn't attainable until systems allow the ceiling to rise for the "big case" side of the practice. Staff meeting time for complex cases is the only way to raise the ceiling of complexity and elevate sales and administrative systems so that the practice can operate at the new level.

Specialists and generalists who spend staff meeting time devoted to marketing and the sales process for their complex cases always see more cases and have more cases going into treatment.

1) They have raised the limit of the ceiling of complexity in the business.

2) They have elevated their abilities and skills to the new ceiling by focusing on systems required for those cases.

3) They likely have deadlines for the systematic changes needed to address "big case"-related systems.

4) They constantly review case-acceptance systems as well as at what point in the system are current prospective cases, resulting in fewer sales-related errors and higher case-acceptance rates.

"Mixed" Practices

Larger multi-doctor teams often operate in a "mixed" practice. One side of the practice handles routine cases and handles a higher volume of patients on an ongoing basis, and the other side of the practice handles the procedures that are more complex or "specialized."

For mixed practices, while a general, monthly team meeting has value, it's important to structure meetings so that systems and routines specific to the success of the "regular" or "complex" practice are addressed. In other words, the teams generally meet separately to focus on what's critical for their success and meet monthly or bimonthly to discuss practice-wide items.

Key Tenet #20

Rehearse and Practice Your Ethical Selling System Consistently

"If you do nothing, you get nothing."—Dr. James McAnally

There are some key reasons why systems, especially those related to systems designed to sell complex things, are necessary and must be reviewed annually.

One of the challenges that professionals such as dentists face is that they spent years learning how to repeat physical steps that create a certain result and these steps continue to be modified as science and technology gradually evolves. They review, rehearse, and adapt to changes.

The same educational process creates a level of perfection and internal motivation that is seldom present outside the licensed professions. It's a human tendency to believe that others are like us in our behaviors. This flawed thinking results in bad management practices where repetition and reinforcement of important skills necessary to maintain proficiency in the team is neglected. It also results in the belief among dentists that, "If I trained the team once on activity X, they'll remember it forever." This is simply not the case.

This thinking results in a lot of practices never reviewing their structured systems for selling their services after the material is covered and implemented the first time. People easily forget important specifics, given enough time, and the result is almost the same as having never gone through the training at all.

The Difference between "Clinical Practice" and "Business "Practice"

There are few clinical settings that do not have two types of practices under the same roof. They have unrelated routines that are mutually exclusive, but they act in tandem to produce the desired result. Patients enjoy life more because of the dental services delivered, and the practices enjoy financial success for the doctors and teams.

Most practices led by a clinician with many hours of advanced education have systems for maintaining clinical knowledge and skills that are repeated on an ongoing basis. It is far easier for the professional to commit to maintaining clinical skills.

Examples are abundant of doctors who devote most of their time acquiring clinical skills and investing (borrowing) large sums to buy clinical equipment. They believe that if they have the skills and equipment, patients will appear, wanting the professional's help, only to find out that this is inaccurate. They spend years digging the practice out of a precarious financial position, or worse, the practice is never financially viable.

Obtaining and maintaining clinical skills is important, but it is also important to remember that the business practice is necessary so that patients can benefit from the clinical practice. Management, marketing, and selling systems all fall under "business practice" to deliver complex services. Ethical Selling (courtesy of selling at appropriate fees and margins due to using a selling system) allows the time to institute and foster the business practices needed.

Only with Mastery Can You Consider Altering a System That Works

Most doctors and teams want to do their tasks at high levels, and they want to improve the way they work. That effort to work at higher levels is part of what keeps life and work interesting. You would be hard pressed to find a dental team that is not looking for better, more reliable ways to help patients have better results, faster, and with less pain.

It's easy to fall into the trap of wanting to improve a process before you have mastered it. The more that a process is outside an individual's training background, the less likely that a random change will actually improve the result.

In athletics, a coach prevents players from changing something without a master's guidance, because unsupervised changes in strategy or technique can easily result in poorer performance. In the dental setting, seldom is a third-party "master" present related to clinical procedures or to a practice system such as selling.

Selling is the most complex process in a practice, especially as case sizes increase. Changes in steps should be considered or instituted only after mastering a selling system. Otherwise, the changes are likely to create worse and frustratingly random results.

Key Tenet #21

Have Ongoing Marketing Meetings with Appropriate Staff

An important skill for any dental business owner is something called "delegated oversight." It's easy to delegate tasks and then never check on progress or actions. The latter is common when someone says, "I gave directions on a project, but nothing happened." Operational trait testing via the Kolbe "A" test (www.Kolbe.com)_ provides information on how the individual will approach routines and tasks both personally and in a work environment. It's important to not only understand the operational traits of your team members but also of yourself since your traits related to starting projects and follow-through can limit progress in the practice just as much as they can from a team member..

As an owner, you can never delegate your role as the "coach" who reviews the game as it is played. No one else will *ever* care about the business as much as you do. As part of delegating but holding others accountable, meet with key team members who are marketing and overseeing sales in the practice. In a small office, those roles might be held by one person, and in larger offices, it could be an entire team. Either way, one-on-one oversight meetings, held weekly, keep these individuals informed and doing the right things.

Your phone staff must be in the loop on the marketing that is active and visible to the public. When patients call about something they've seen about the practice, and the front office personnel acts as if they have no idea what the patient is talking about, doubt is planted in the patient's mind. Watch your own behavior when you interact with a business that has done something to stimulate your interest but "drops the ball" when you call to find out more.

For large practices, consider a dedicated marketing assistant to handle the routines of buying ads and changing strategies based on the time of year. Even with a marketing assistant, weekly meetings with the "coach" are still necessary.

Key Tenet #22

Constantly Identify, Reduce, and Eliminate Barriers to Treatment

The ten greatest patient barriers (risks) to significant dental treatment are as follows:

1. Time

2. Money

3. Spouse, significant other, financial veto holder

4. Societal beliefs (influence of others)

5. Treatment outcome

6. Fear (past experience, past imagined experience, current fear)

7. Don't see, hear, or feel a need

8. Too many choices

9. Expectations (What will I look like? How will it work? How long will it last?)

10. Psychological issues

"Only a fool learns from his mistakes, I prefer to learn from the mistakes of others."—Otto Von Bismarck

This list of barriers is one of the best regarding what those with advanced training can and can't do in practice. It took years to recognize the issues that frequently affect patient decision making and can prevent a decision to have treatment.

Almost universally, if you ask a trained dentist, "What's the main issue with patients deciding on care and going forward or not going forward?" the top answer will be "money" or "patient financing."

While finances always play into treatment decisions, this answer is too simplistic and reveals a clinician who hasn't spent much time (or any) as a serious student of patient behavior. The clinician hasn't thought about the barriers that are just as likely to affect treatment decisions as the one he or she pins the blame on.

Why should you be concerned about these barriers? If you agree that your patients are far better off when they get their dental health back for chewing, social purposes, and self-esteem, that there are likely direct health benefits or reduced risk for serious systemic health problems, and that the people around the patient are better off (family, coworkers, kids, spouse), it's your professional duty to identify and remove barriers to treatment, so that your patients have the ability to choose what is best for their lifestyle, comfort, or appearance.

Because many barriers leading to "no" are identifiable, by looking for and addressing them, the odds of gaining acceptance greatly increase. Systematic identification is possible only if a selling process (system) is followed. Michael Gerber, author of 'The E-Myth' ranks sales systems as the most important soft system in any business ("soft" meaning unrelated to the physical facility). It is shocking how many dentists have read E-myth and believe in the concepts yet refuse to develop or to seek out a system already developed for selling professional services. [Details on how to start using just such a systematic approach for selling professional services in an ethical manner is discussed on the last page of this book.]

Besides getting in the way of a patient having the benefits of twenty-first-century dental technology, materials, and methods, unidentified and unaddressed barriers automatically mean rejection. No one likes to hear the word no. From a sales standpoint, hearing "no" hinders your team's confidence in presenting your cases well, impacts how you feel about what you are selling, and affects how successful you are at case acceptance/actual sales. The more you hear "yes," the more likely you will continue to do so. The same holds true if you hear "no" more often than not! It is important to address the barriers because of the damage caused by hearing more no's than necessary.

While the top ten barriers remained the same, the Great Recession altered consumer behavior. How long does it take for a behavior to permanently change? A recent study done in the UK showed that, depending on complexity, a new habit or behavior can form between 18 and 254 days. (Lally, P., van Jaarsveld, C. H. M., Potts, H. W. W., & Wardle, J. (2010). How are habits formed: Modeling habit formation in the real world. *European Journal of Social Psychology, 40,* 998-1009) The extended period of economic disruption changed many people's habits including how they decide to spend. For the foreseeable future, consumers are buying less "stuff." In every income category, less "stuff" will have an upside of prioritizing health-oriented decisions over "things."

Regardless of an individual's behavior changes or new habits related to spending, borrowing, or saving, the economic "norm" of credit, jobs, wage growth, and financial health following the recession has made it more important than ever to have qualifying steps early in the case-acceptance process. This reduces the time spent on patients who don't have, or can't find, the financial resources for elective treatment.

While the barrier dentists most frequently cite as an issue (money) that impedes patients from opting for better care, any one of the ten barriers is as likely to be present and as likely to derail a complex case from going into treatment. With appropriate qualifying steps built into your system for selling, the majority of patients to whom you present treatment to can likely accept at least one of the treatment plans proposed. For a well-qualified patient, the final barrier, beyond a decision to spend money on treatment, will likely involve other issues on the list. Routinely ask yourself, "What is it about this patient's situation, beyond willingness to spend money that could negatively impact a decision for treatment?"

Is there a way to have permanent, one hundred percent case acceptance and one hundred percent barrier elimination? It is possible, in a finite period, to have one hundred percent case acceptance even with elective dentistry in the tens of thousands of dollars per case. Several of our Academy members have proven this. However, beyond a limited timeframe, the answer is no. Once the case fee is $10,000 or more, even with Ethical Selling, the acceptance range averages 35–70 percent.

As "sales maturity" progresses, the surprise at what can "blow up" a case goes away. As you think about the top barriers, and as patients march through the case-acceptance system, patterns become clear. Even for the no's, it's important to analyze what happened so that you can improve your chances when a similar situation arises. Address the ten barriers, and you'll automatically put more of those advanced skills to work.

Key Tent #23

"The Decider" or Other Financial Stakeholder(s) Must Be at the Case Presentation

"The Decider" or other financial stakeholders play a big role in patient decision making when it comes to major dental treatment. In many situations, the decider other individuals may have the final word on whether the patient can make a decision to have their situation treated.

That person is the second (and sometimes third) individual who has major input into financial decisions and whether a case goes forward. Beyond the financial decision makers, there are also opinionated friends and family, who can impact patient decision making both positively and negatively. However, if the financial decider is left out of treatment discussions, you'll never have the luxury of dealing with these other individuals.

Who is this decider? Most of the time, it's the spouse or a boyfriend or girlfriend. Coming in a close second is the parent of an adult child or an adult child of a senior parent. Trustees are a very distant third.

This person's position is so important in the decision making process that it's essential to reserve a spot for him or her on the tracking system you use to follow your cases through your selling process.

One of the former hosts of 'The Tonight Show', Johnny Carson, regularly performed a comedy skit called Carnac the Magnificent. He'd hold a sealed envelope over his Turban, worn for the occasion, and predict an answer to the question contained in the envelope which was some joke play on an individual or current events topic. If your patient's "decider" is not present at the time of discussion when major treatment is being presented, here's a prediction of what you'll hear from your patient: "I have to go home and talk about it with _____ (insert the decider's name)." Unfortunately, there's no joke attached to this accurate prediction since the patient will have a very difficult time conveying what has been discussed. In the majority of cases, when this individual is absent, what could have been a decision to correct a major dental problem will be pushed to the way side simply because this individual was not at the appointment.

Without adherence to a checklist ensuring that steps are followed in your selling process, including finding out who the financial decider(s) are and making sure they are part of treatment discussions and, in some cases, even present at examination appointments, the decider is routinely absent. One program alumnus, seeing a distinct drop off in case acceptance, found that the practice/doctor/team eliminated the decider at the case presentation. It was no surprise that this resulted in the financial detriment of the practice and the health detriment of the patients!

You realize that you are working with pros when you observe a "big ticket" item sales process and the product/service's decider issue is handled early in the sales. This individual is seamlessly made a part of the process from the beginning, so when the point of decision arrives, the person is present.

In dentistry, the neophyte solution to the problem is to deny it and keep presenting without the decider present. Ninety-five percent of practices do this, and it's not only does this hinder their results, but it hurts patient health.

Others, upon realizing that the decider's absence is going to be an issue, will make ineffective attempts in the final days (sometimes hours) before the treatment discussion appointment to get the decider involved. Springing such a request late in the process reduces, or destroys, the trust built. Furthermore, surprises activate automatic choosing systems or "gut instinct" as discussed by Columbia professor Dr. Sheena Iyengar. These instincts tell us to say "no" to requests automatically when confronted with the unexpected. A response that over-rides rational thought.

There are presenters who from the lecture podium encourage the profession to "man-up" at case presentation with admonitions that when the patient response is "I've got to go home and think/talk it over with my spouse, etc." that the sales "response" is to What? Aren't you an adult? Can't you make a decision on your own?" While perhaps such a route is worthy of selling someone on a gym membership, I encourage you to let science show you the high road on dealing with patient instincts that can help or hinder them from embarking on life changing treatment.

The best solution in the "decider" issue is to make it a matter of fact that the decider will join your team and the patient at case presentation and give them the reasons why.

Why is "why" so important?

Harvard psychologist and Association for Psychological Science fellow Dr. Ellen Langer documented rule-based human behavior in a study in the 1970's where researchers asked if they could cut in line to use a copy machine. When they said, "Excuse me. May I use the copy machine?" only 60 percent of the subjects complied (meaning that 40 percent said, "No, you can't cut in line, wait your turn"). When the researchers gave a reason—"Excuse me. May I use the copy machine because I'm in a rush?"—94 percent of the subjects agreed. Believing there must be some mistake; researchers repeated the test again with the phrase, "Excuse me. May I use the copy machine because I need to make some copies?" This time an unbelievable 93 percent of the subjects agreed despite the fact that "I need to make some copies" is not a good reason for cutting in line. (Langer, E., Blank, A., & Chanowitz, B. (1978). The mindlessness of Ostensibly Thoughtful Action: The Role of "Placebic" Information in Interpersonal Interaction. *Journal of Personality and Social Psychology, 36(6),* 635-642.

Another behaviorist, Dr. Robert Cialdini, states that "when people hear the word *because*, they assume that there must be a good reason." That magic word is the shortcut people use to distinguish between good arguments and bad.

If you provide valid reasons that it's important to the patient and decider to be at the appropriate appointments, based on our member surveys, roughly 94% will join you at the case presentation appointment.

"What are several 'whys' for your situation? Here are a few.

Your spouse (husband, anyone who will be involved financially) needs to be at this visit

"Because what we will be talking about is complicated, and there is no simple way for you to go home and explain what's going to work best with getting you back to (insert solution here).

"The decision to have this kind of dentistry impacts every part of your life and it's a big financial decision.

For those with active periodontal disease): "Because the dental problem you have is infectious, we need to have both of you here to discuss how to get healthy again."

In practices new to these concepts, the doctor will be resistant to putting into place appropriate, systematic steps to get the decider involved, or the staff will be resistant. Either way, this step has to be included. The evidence is in.

A concept often discussed in the ethical selling program taught to Academy members is that your patient will fill in any blanks you leave in the treatment discussion or selling process with answers that you won't like.

As part of a structured, systematic, selling process it's important to put what's expected from the patient and the decider by the practice in writing and include reinforcement of this in your verbal discussions ("here's what happens at your first, second, and third visit") along with a list of "whys." Your patients will have a better chance of making a decision to do something good for themselves.

If you leave out "because," you are throwing away case acceptance and underserving your prospective patients.

Key Tenet #24

Create a "Public" Personality, and Make Yourself a Mini-Celebrity

Take a look at this list:

1. Michael Jackson
2. Twilight
3. WWE (World Wrestling Entertainment)
4. Megan Fox
5. Britney Spears
6. Naruto (Japanese anime)
7. American Idol
8. Kim Kardashian
9. NASCAR
10. Runescape

These are the most popular internet searches for the first decade of the 2000s. Weekly search items changes as the names and news stories work their way through the Internet search engine queries. There are a handful of "personalities" who work to maintain themselves near the top of the list. Britney Spears and Paris Hilton are two prominent examples.

Whether it's a presidential race or a race to watch a new reality TV show, the world loves celebrity action. Celebrities leverage their personal brand to make them different from others around them, bring attention to themselves, and get more work.

"Painless Parker" comes to mind for equivalent of a top-ten dental "celebrity." He likely had the highest recognition ever among dentists, and that was a century ago when telegrams were the main forms of communication.

To ensure that you don't get caught up in thinking that creating bigger than reality celebrity image is a modern invention of the entertainment industry consider Thomas Alvin Edison.

While nothing can be taken for granted about historical education, the odds are that practically reading this has a passing knowledge of who Edison was and what he (and a teams of hired engineers) invented and took credit for developing.

Fourteen of the companies Edison founded are still with us including Consolidated-Edison (ConEd) and General Electric. Many of his inventions were considered much less superior than other devices on the market, but they still sold more units, proving that the famous quote by R. W. Emerson holds little truth: "Build a better mousetrap, and the world will beat a path to your door." Edison was keen on making sure that his name was associated with the consumer products he invented and his companies made and distributed because by doing so he helped the consumer decide to buy his version of a product. The conversation occurring in a household of that period can easily be imagined "We have an Edison phonograph—remember, we read about him in *Life* last week? There's also this other Edison model coming. I think he must know what he's doing."

Now Britney, Paris and countless others understand and crave celebrity for their business interests. While some crave celebrity on an unimaginable level, even "regular people" far away from Hollywood desire some modicum of celebrity. Examples abound, particularly in fundraising athletic events. In its Susan G. Komen Race for the Cure Series, Nike keeps track of the participants who raise the requested amount of funds and puts their names on the windows of stores in the cities where the events are held. Runners, family members, and friends scour the walls looking for their name in tiny type and snapping photos. It's "your name in lights" on a small scale and celebrity on the smallest scale.

For large cases (larger treatment plans and cost), patients want to trust someone that many others trust. This trust is bolstered by patient testimonials and doctor endorsements and mini-celebrity status can further strengthen the message these items carry to prospective patients considering you and your practice.

Here are the fundamentals of being a "celebrity":

- Put more of your personal life (activities, vacations, family, crazy relatives, interests, hobbies, sports) in your newsletters and on your website. Patients find those things far more interesting than the latest technical advancement.

- The more they hear your story, the more they see you as different from other dentists (the boring ones).

- Using "you" as the brand in marketing greatly bumps up the celebrity factor. You're paying for marketing, so why not allow it to provide more benefit?

- Actual stories about you and your practice in local media create mini-celebrity, regardless of whether the stories are created as a by-product of advertising relationships with local media.

Key Tenet #25

Wise Use of Patient Success Stories

This is the second-most underutilized secret in the profession when it comes to accumulating advantages in the marketplace. The consumer is overburdened with choices of all kinds be it with the jeans they wear, vacations they take, or what they choose at the aisles of the local grocery store. As decisions become more complex they crave direction on choosing and look for shortcuts that help them with decision making.

As an example on how consumers and patients are looking for shortcuts with deciding, the words "review" and "scan" often follow searches for products or services. Internet searches are the modern day equivalent of a "backyard fence" where prospective patients ask questions about procedures and providers from their neighbors. They want to know what other people are saying, doing, and choosing. The practitioner who provides the most stories has a major advantage in these indirect conversations that patients have with other people considering your services.

Here's what goes on in a patient's head after reviewing an encyclopedic mass of patient success stories: "If 89 patients are happy with their reconstruction, cosmetic dentistry, cosmetic denture, or sedation dentistry by Dr. Golden Hands with that Awesome Smile, I'm probably happy with my treatment too."

How Are Customers Doing This Research?

- ◆ Your website

- ◆ Google

- ◆ Business review sites (Yelp, Google, YP, Yahoo, etc.)

- ◆ The materials they get from you directly when inquiring about services

The unspoken question is this: "Do these messages sync with what I'm seeing, hearing, and reading?' The higher the cost of treatment, the more likely that the research phase will be intensive with investigating what others are saying about your services

Instinct plays a role. Behavioral science shows that people follow their instincts when deciding to save time and reduce complexity. If something is out of sync, our hardwired reflex protects us.

While in some ways this ability to research you truly give "power to the people," you can fill in some of the items needed to help patients with their decision making from information about services to academic background and via providing personal stories shared by your patients as part of their treatment. You can influence the "conversation" occurring around your practice as it relates to you, your team, and services more than at any other time in history.

Gathering patient "success stories" must be systematized during and after treatment. Update files as the stories are captured, or hold interviews (written, audio, or video) and update them quarterly.

Making the testimonial an expected part of treatment during case presentations is highly recommended. This way, you set the stage for the best testimonials: "Mrs. Jones, if we do everything we say we'll do, we expect that you'll be willing to let us tell other people your story."

Be sure to have a script or checklist to get a heartfelt story once treatment is done. Otherwise, you'll be stuck with dozens of testimonials that are little better than "the doc's great!"

Here are examples of the types of questions that belong on a success story checklist:

- What was life like before?

- What were previous dental experiences like?

- What about now?

- How do you feel now as compared to then?

- Are you glad you had _____ performed?

- What would you like to share with someone else considering the same treatment?

Videotaped Testimonials

Written testimonials are good, but professional video of your best patient stories is the "Ferrari" of testimonials.

With Internet video content, quality has moved well beyond the "home recorder" level. Plan to solicit and convene a cross-section of 12-20 of your patients who are the happiest with a variety of clinical treatment performed by you and your team on a day to professionally capture their stories.

The patients who have experienced the biggest benefits and life changes are routinely the ones that want to share what's possible with other potential patients. They will often feel honored to ask to be captured on video. Professionally captured and edited video testimonials can have an impact in helping other patients decide on treatment options for 10-15 years before requiring an update.

The following is an example of a patient success story. It's not great but is significantly above and beyond what most dentists garner from their patients. Note that the full patient name, age, location, and occupation all add to the power of the story.

"Let me tell you how the process of going from an upper denture and a few lower working teeth with a partial went for me. Every few years or so, I would have a lower tooth flare up on me and give me really bad toothaches, where my tooth would hurt for days and keep me up at night. Sometimes it would even swell up, and as a chiropractor, you can imagine how bad that looks to my own patients. I knew after years of neglect that it was time to start taking care of my dental health, so I searched the web and found Dr. xxxx's office. After my initial visit, I knew this was the place for me.

"After my first and only big surgery, I was sore for a couple of days, but I had pain pills to take care of that. It was on a Thursday, and I was back to work and functioning fine by the following Monday! That was great to not have to miss any work. Plus I haven't been in any pain the last two months with these temporary denture healing teeth. I never realized what a thorn my teeth used to be and how they were affecting my life in a negative way. I was always in pain. For the last thirty years, I've been dealing with constant pain and infection in my body from my teeth. It's amazing how much better my body has felt since I got my old infected teeth out of my body. I sleep better, don't have ear aches anymore, and my appetite is up! I'm so much happier in general. I never realized how big of an impact my teeth could have on my happiness in life!" Gary Gallow, 63, Whidbey Island Chiropractor

Key Tenet #26

Wise Use of Third-Party Endorsements

This is the most underutilized secret in the profession. It's pointless to brag about your traits yourself. Most societies dislike a bragger. Unless you're doing veterinary dentistry on the side, all of your patients are human. It's human nature to roll your eyes anytime someone says "I'm the best" at anything. (Muhammad Ali as exception to the rule.) A number of dental boards prohibit you from explicitly stating that you are clinically better than anyone else. There are almost no restrictions on what patients and other professionals can say as it attests to your skill level. Here are some examples.

Colleague endorsements. Endorsements by fellow colleagues build credibility and trust. They can be used throughout their practice and in external marketing. Be aware that any credentials discussed in an endorsement mean little to the average patient unless they are written about in a way that states why the credential is important.

The goal of gathering colleague endorsements is to create the following in the patient's mind: "Gee, this dentist is endorsed by quite a few colleagues and I don't see anyone endorsing this other dentist, that's enough for me to give them a call."

A few states prohibit a doctor from giving an endorsement to another doctor or product in the state of license but usually do not prohibit doctors outside the state from doing so.

Labs. Endorsement by reputable dental laboratories can lend additional credibility as the lab is intimately aware of your services and the cases crossing their benches. If you work with a specific lab on many of your complex cases, the lab will likely write an endorsement if asked, which covers from their view why prospective patients should trust you.

Classmates. For doctors not affiliated with our Programs, gaining endorsements from classmates that reside in other cities is an option to build the strength of your third-party messages. These of course will be classmates that you have confidence in their clinical skills since it's likely you will cross-endorse their skills. Feel free to suggest this book to them if they want to better understand what to do with their endorsement.

Publications. When a practice receives media exposure, such as an interview in a local publication, or by purchasing print space for "advertorial"-style advertisement, there is an opportunity to turn the interview or advertorial into an endorsement. The public believes what it sees in print to be "news," and news automatically lends itself to third-party credibility.

Other professionals. The public looks to professionals for guidance about other professionals: lawyers, accountants, architects, engineers, physicians, and dentists. Endorsements from this other professionals carry some weight when patients are deciding on your services. Because it is may be hard to visualize what a fellow professional would say in endorsing your services,

Advanced Third-Party Endorsements: Using and Creating News about You to Promote a VIP—You!

Here is more information on how to use an advanced type of third-party endorsement that "puts you in the news" and in the minds of the consumer and prospective patient.

Anyone familiar with the movie *Avatar* may know about the records it set; some were a by-product of technology, and other records resulted from the studio leveraging one success to another. The film received major kudos in the press for the advances in computer-generated images that created scenery unlike anything seen before. It was almost the equivalent of the breakthroughs in cinematography when *Gone with the Wind* was filmed. Ticket sales have finally eclipsed even Scarlett and Rhett's sales, which in an inflation adjusted terms would be $1.5 billion in today's dollars.

Time reviewed the movie, describing what the viewer would experience thanks to new filming technologies, and did a good job of painting a picture of the storyline. The review was something film studios wish they could buy, but when that kind of a review happens, it is typically wasted after the single "flash" it shines onto the film.

With *Avatar*, something smart occurred following the *Time* review. The studio didn't do what was the industry norm, grabbing a four- or five-word "printed bite" from the review and displaying it as a by-line the next advertisement showing a photo of the movie poster but took a major chunk of the entire review and turned it into "news" about the movie itself (prefaced with large print declaring that "*Time* says").

An interview-style ad (or advertorial) in a local publication, can do the same for you. It allows you to create the appearance that the Local News Daily is saying, "Pay attention to the following important information about Dr. Jones."

Local publications can be interested in interviewing you if you are first to bring some new technology, treatment, or facility to the area. That is the ideal scenario but an infrequent one. In the grand scheme of things, dentistry is seen as a low-interest story by most reporters and editors. If you are fortunate enough to garner such an interview, the interview demands repurposing as news about the practice and doctor (just as the studio repurposed its "news" from the *Time* review of *Avatar*).

Because interviews about practices are few and far between, it is up to the practice to create its own news and leverage this concept. There are two ways to create your "news."

Hire a freelance writer to write an advertorial about what the practice wants to convey or buy ad space and simply ask that the newspaper interview you and create an advertorial with the help of someone on the staff.

Create the advertorial or expand on one from another industry.

- Pay attention to promotional efforts in other or larger cities while traveling.

- Watch for advertorials in national newspapers. Considerable time and expense will have gone into the production of these ads.

- Look for example advertorials seen in the inflight magazines during air travel.

Following publication, use the advertorial to create the "news" affect and another level of third-party endorsement:

Excerpt chunks of the original advertorial and create an ad similar to what the studio did for *Avatar*

- Start with the headline of the name of the local paper then place the advertorial "news" below it.Shrink the advertorial and add a new border and headline such as "*Detroit Times* Discusses Local Dentist Solving Dental Problem ABC."

Most newspapers will require the word "advertisement" at the top so as not to confuse the reader into thinking that the newspaper endorsed the ad as editorial content. Regardless of that disclaimer, the fact that something is in print means that it's news to most readers.

The "news" can be recycled into other locations: the materials for your reception area, the walls of the office, operatories, and consultation room, and in information and consultation packets.

Key Tenet #27

Prevent "Fee Shock" and Patient/Doctor Embarrassment

Patients don't magically know what dentistry costs or should cost. The following conversations were heard at a major dental meeting:

"Patients are always surprised when we present fees to them."

"The other day, a patient left my office crying once she heard the fees."

"My staff is scared to present anything over $3,000 to a patient because we've lost patients before with treatment plans that large."

These statements were overheard at chair side:

"I didn't know it would cost that much!"

"I'm not spending that much!"

"You're ripping me off!"

"Fee shock" is typically thought as being a one-way street and blames the patient for not knowing what things cost. While some responsibility does reside with the customer to investigate the price of goods and services, there is plenty of room for improvement in being more up-front about potential costs.

A third party listening to the conversations surmises that the recipient (the patient) has little idea of what significant dentistry costs and that most providers (dentist and practice) are doing an inadequate job of reducing what is a recurring "surprise" in most practices.

In the public sphere, there isn't that much information around regarding dental costs compared to, say, the real estate or new cars section in the paper, and few dentists provide the correct fee related information that set the tone for fee discussions.. Most fear revealing fees or are embarrassed by their own fees.

"Fee shock" is a big problem. It is up there with the top recurring themes: pain, time, and insurance are the only others that equal or surpass it. These are what patients ask about, what dentists know will be asked about, and what dentists agree create the biggest barriers to patients making good decisions. You can expect almost all four to occur every day the door of the practice is unlocked or the telephone is answered!

In baseball, this would be the equivalent of the pitcher having only four pitches to throw. Imagine what batting averages would be! Dentists know that there is a high likelihood of repeatable "pitches" (including the "surprise" over fees) being thrown, and yet most are caught off guard by them.

The best solutions for talking to patients who are ready to hear your fee, and avoiding sticker shock, include these:

- Use the Master Dentist Academy's "Fee Framing" concept. That includes written materials that are part of financial screening and qualifying, presenting verbally during diagnostics as part of the practice's systematic approach to Ethical Selling, and presenting verbally in hygiene related to choices or next steps besides "just a cleaning."

- Understand the psychology behind pricing.
- Present fees in a specific manner at case presentation.

Key Tenet #28

Present Fees Correctly

How fees are presented makes a big difference in results, yet the majority of dentists would fail the simplest test about the matter. As a result, more patients get "the short end of the stick" and wind up with dental options that aren't as good for them. That is the travesty of behavioral science not being brought into the dental office.

Who knew that if you delivered a range of pricing options from lowest cost to highest, or from highest to lowest, it affected the consumer's buying decision?

This phenomenon was recognized in the sales world before science statistically validated it. Robert Cialdini's "law of concessions," described in his seminal book 'Influence: Science and Practice,' is defined as an individual being more likely and willing to say yes to a given request (including a presented fee) if another significantly larger request is made first and then immediately following the larger request a smaller lesser request is then made. In *The Art of Choosing*, Dr. Sheena Iyengar spends considerable time discussing pricing and the effect on choice, detailing the studies that further validate Cialdini's law.

When this law of behavior is ignored by a doctor and team, patients are automatically more likely to choose options that are worse for them. It could be deemed un-ethical to understand the power of these laws regarding how humans choose related to price and then willingly present treatments and prices so that a patient makes a choice that is worse for their health.

If you or your spouse has ever stepped into an upper mid-level retailer or luxury retailer, you'll find this science applied at every turn. Some products may or may not be great for the buyer or offer any life-changing potential, but the retail world applies the science for its benefit. Pay close attention in these environments, and you will find with most items at least one ultra-high-priced version of a product near other items that are similar yet priced at 5 percent to 10 percent of the other item.

A number of years ago, you could find a $14,000 women's handbag at Coach, a U.S. luxury bag maker, next to a $700 model. This is a direct example of the stage being set so that Cialdini's law of concessions comes into play even in the absence of a sales person discussing pricing. Consumers see the low-priced item next to the high-priced item, and this raises the threshold of what they are willing to pay for a "regular" purse. Without the higher-priced product, the other products would not sell for as much. Coach and other retailers continue to press the limits of what 'expensive' is simply because the law of concessions cares little about what the price is that sets the tone for the concession request.

For the dentist offering complex services, the law of concessions shows that there must always be a treatment plan option that is more costly than the others. By its very existence, the more costly treatment makes the patient likely to choose other less costly options. In other words, a better choice is made thanks to a mention of a high-cost option first.

It should also be noted that in Cialdini's research, if the smaller request was made first (e.g. fee, price, or task), the odds of a larger request (e.g. higher fee, higher price, or larger task) being accepted was significantly lower than when the order was reversed

This concept of presenting the highest fee option first is a powerful way to tie-in and to emphasize loss when lesser options are discussed. In any endeavor where a choice is being made, while it's fine to talk about gain, it should be the lesser of the discussions.

Here is some example language: "With option C, you lose these benefits." "With option B, here's what you don't get." That loss-related language results in a better choice related to good treatment plans.

There are other additional fee factors to consider. For any treatment beyond one tooth, bundle fees. An unbundled fee creates complexity, and complexity kills decision making. When a patient demands a fee breakdown, limit the breakdown to pretreatment, surgical treatment, restorative/reconstructive treatment, post treatment, and perhaps a management fee (if one dentist is coordinating multi-provider treatment).

Key Tenet #29

Leadership and Believability Impact
Acceptance and Price

It's always best if teams present one fee for each case option even though multiple doctors may be involved.

Think about how much more complexity and confusion come automatically if three different treating practices present fees on different days after much overly technical discussion.

It's best that one of the practices closes the case and moves the patient into treatment even in a team treatment setting where a generalist and one or more specialists are involved. Whoever has the most experience in presenting cases must take over this aspect, be it the specialist or generalist. Forget egos, close the case according to the principles discussed in this book and taught in our ethical selling program, and help the patient. It's OK for the dentist closing the cases to have compensation in the overall case fee for being the expert at helping patients choose their options according to the behavioral science.

With larger cases (treatment above a certain level as you define that; for most dentists, $3,000 to $5,000 constitutes "big"), it is best if the person who is trusted the most (the doctor) presents the treatment plan fees. Financial arrangements are then made by the team member responsible for doing so and in a systematized fashion.

If the doctor cannot be trained to be a great "fee presenter," someone else on the team must become great at it. Otherwise, a case-size ceiling will be reached no matter how much skill the doctor and team have.

Key Tenet #30

Offer a Warranty or "Our Promise"

We move on to the why's and how's related to warranties (or promises for doctors practicing in California) in the dental practice.

Warranty Reality

The majority of practices provide implied dental warranties, meaning that if something breaks, the patient expects a repair or replacement. While most in the profession buy into the implied warranty, few leverage the power of the warranty itself to help patients decide to move forward with treatment options. The best way to do so is to understand that there is a both power and good reason to move from an implied warranty to one more explicit and detailed about what can be expected from the dentistry performed for a defined period following treatment. It also provides direction on what is expected by the patient after the completion of major dentistry.

Not only do most practices not put the power of the warranty to work, under the implied warranty plan, they leave themselves open to providing free services well beyond what is a reasonable period. They lose out on putting some responsibility, based on behaviors and actions, on the patient. They get few of the true benefits but assume most of the risk. If you already provide an implied warranty, why not put it in writing, use it to your advantage, and allow it to help more patients choose better treatment?

Here are more reasons that this makes sense:

- Compared to other surrounding practices, a well-publicized warranty creates a difference between your practice and others. You can go as far as developing a warranty that no one else has.

- It contributes to creating your "category of one."

- It is a significant component of allowing service pricing that is no longer based purely on lowest cost comparisons with other practices because the message is explicit. The warranty is included with this fee.

- It limits what you will and won't warranty, for how long, and the patient's role in keeping the warranty valid (including defining patient responsibility while defining future clinical risk based on patient history).

For times when retreatment is given at no charge (it happens in every practice), the patients are reminded that the service was performed under warranty and that is one reason that they came to see you.

There are some caveats before jumping feet first into "Warranty Land":

1. Your fees must be high enough so you can afford to repair or replace dentistry when it doesn't work as expected. Deeply discounted services are hard to warranty since there is little to no reserve to handle replacement or repair. If you can't sell at appropriate fees, resolve that issue first.

2. In the warranty stipulations include a sentence about non-transferability and termination if you cease to practice, become disabled, or retire. The document should be reviewed by an attorney licensed in your state or province.

Key Tenet #31

Use Appropriate "Case-Acceptance" Technology

In dentistry, the term "sales" was supplanted by "case acceptance." That diversion into a dubious place semantically has led to generations of confused dentists who do not understand that they are selling.

As a result, the paths charted for "selling" in dentistry have led thousands of us far away from reality. We wander lost in a "case-acceptance" desert, a land inhabited by vendors and consultants of false messages, academics who have never sold a thing, and expensive equipment, all geared toward gaining and proclaiming "case acceptance" at major dental meetings.

Do a quick review of the chapter titles in this book and the fundamentals for success at marketing and ethically selling your dentistry. Almost none relate to a complicated technology. Return mentally to the dental trade-show or association sponsored meeting, and you'll find vendor aisles packed with an array of high-tech software packages and "educational" products, all promising case-acceptance nirvana.

Dentists are natural-born gadget and widget types, which means that they are easy prey for technology based solutions. "Simply install the software, and push play, or drag this model or giant flip chart in front of the patient, run to operatory 2 and perform some dentistry, and when you come back, voila, the patient has been hypnotized into saying 'yes, doctor' to necessary treatment." Everybody is happy in fantasy land back in the manufacturer aisles trade show until the purchase arrives at the dental operatory, and for some strange reason, the theoretical result isn't happening.

Even worse, a number of big-ticket equipment manufacturers (cone-beam computed tomography vendors and chair-side milling machines makes being the most recent culprits) weave "case-acceptance" promises into their product pitches. Most patients are radiology enthusiasts in their spare time, right? What patient doesn't lie awake wondering which "Cerec" dentist they'll seek out on Monday morning?

It's not only the equipment vendors pushing such a message. Examine the next salvo of dental magazine-catalogs, and you'll find plenty of claims for even lower-priced widgets that someone the widget influences decisions by patients without any skill or knowledge of the doctor and team. One major mass-market consultant (the name rhymes with "codger") had full-page ads claiming that a specific type of laser directly created more case acceptance. It would be truthful to discuss how an understanding of pricing and behavior is a must when adding costly technologies that will effective the service mix and price of services. In other words, the reverse of what is being presented. Our Academy members understand that simply owning any kind of device does not create a decision to purchase care. The smartest would point out that a financial relationship between said laser and the consultant is a near certainty. This entanglement and confusion certainly results in more equipment moving off the shelves. The reps are skilled at getting "equipment acceptance" from the dentist. Invariably, some of the doctors who fall for this case-acceptance message will be put on the financial rocks, sometimes even insolvency, because a machine was put ahead of systematically selling first.

Want a needle to pop the "hype balloon" of whether or not a technology will be helpful with case acceptance? Great! Here it is. The question that cuts straight to the point about a technology and its impact on patients deciding to enter treatment is this: "Does X decrease complexity for someone of average or less-than-average intelligence and improve the basic understanding of the problem or solution?" If the answer is yes, it's worth investigating how the technology could plug into your structured sales process. If not, "pop the balloon" and move on to something more important.

In a world where the total amount of information is expanding at a rate of 66 percent per year (and it doubles every eighteen months), the complexity of living and making choices, for anyone not stranded on a desert island, is going up. Production of physical goods expansion hovers at 2–3 percent per year in Western economies and 7 percent per year in developing ones. Anything that simplifies life is a relief to the consumer.

What technologies make a real difference when it comes to helping patients understand proposed treatments? Most of the items hawked at trade shows can be left to gather dust. The technology that affects case acceptance the most, hands down, is imaging or simulations, but the majority of dental practices don't do these even when discussing anterior cosmetic dentistry! Some invest in software packages for this purpose, but the doctor is the only person who knows how to manipulate the images. This adds more on the doctor's "plate," which is the last thing to do in a practice beyond the start-up phase when there are few patients and mostly "down" time with empty operatories. This added task falls to the wayside quickly. Others brush off this concept because they let apply their technical eye for detail in the same manner as if the simulation was the actual restoration. As a result, something that is important for the patient and that helps them understand and decide is disregarded and as a result patients understand less and choose less beneficial options. Everyone loses when imaging isn't done. Do yourself a favor and go to SmileVision.net.

The Technologies that Contribute to Patients Making Better Decisions

- **"What if" simulations.** These are a must for anything that changes the appearance of teeth and for replacing even a single tooth. How many "build your own" design tools do you find on the Internet? What about downloadable screen savers or wallpaper images of products? You name it, and you can configure it, color it, or print it out so that you can imagine owning it. As a reminder, you are in an 'unfair' competition with a lot of other major goods that compete for interest and for the same decision making on how and what an individual is going to spend money for their wants and needs. It's hard to not find a product that may cost as much as major dentistry that doesn't allow the prospective buyer to "simulate" the version of the product they would like to own. *In your practice, if it is an elective procedure and requires an expense of more than a $1,000, image it so the patient can see what they are buying.*

- **Digital photos.** Use these to illustrate problems and solutions in a simple manner, using simple language. Patients don't understand *caries*, but they understand *severe cavity* and *bone infection*. Many simple programs allow you to open, draw, and type onto digital photos to point out what you see in terms that patients can understand.

- **Educational software.** This is not that powerful for convincing someone to move forward with treatment, but it is helpful for improving efficiency for the time needed for conveying basic information about problems and procedures. It is especially helpful in bringing "financial others" up to speed about the information. In most cases, the critical co-decider (or decider) arrives much less familiar with the problem than the patient and usually well after the consultation and diagnostic appointments.

- **PowerPoint presentations.** These are helpful when divided into segments: Here's where you are now, here are the options, and here's what you will look like. For the advanced, music can be added to the presentation based on the patient's preferences previously discerned as part of the practice's selling system. These allow the patient and decider to view the "here's where you are now" segment and a simulation at the end of the presentation while a staff member is present, carefully observing reactions. This should happen before the doctor arrives to continue the case presentation. Any information of value is verbally passed to the doctor by the staff member before the doctor enters the room.

- **Big monitors.** Make the "difficult to see" highly visible with a big display. Remember those quaint devices called intra-oral cameras? They were all about putting something small on a "giant" 12-inch TV monitor. With 32-inch monitors now selling for $400, any practice not using a "big screen" to create much higher levels of understanding is missing the boat.

- **X-rays.** Think carefully about which images can be made understandable. When illustrated very simply (teeth that are not savable crossed out, decay noted in red, where bone should be and where it is now, etc.), x-rays can be helpful. Panoramic and 3-D images can be more helpful.

Key Tenet #32

Don't Let Context (Facility) Sabotage Acceptance or Fees

What do Coldwater Creek, Williams-Sonoma, Starbucks, and Apple have in common? The answers that come to mind for most people are nice products and higher-than-average prices. Here is an even more important question. What business characteristics do they all have in common? The top commonalities include the following:

1. All four have physical environments designed to communicate and get premium pricing above similar products in the same categories. That is why Apple has a margin of 32 percent and Best Buy is at 1 percent.

2. The selling environment and routines for selling are structured differently than others in the same niches. This allows margin to stay well above the industry average.

3. Management is committed to do what it takes to keep greater-than-industry margins. The product, service, and context for selling bring a slew of side effects, including ongoing remodels and refreshing the selling environment faster than competitors.

These allow for a long-term advantage and better environment for selling versus competitors and continued motivation to "out-innovate" due to a higher margin and better rewards for everyone in the company. The result is outselling others, at a better margin, even though essentially bringing a similar product to the consumer. Is an Apple computer worth two or three times more than a Dell? It depends on who you ask. There are enough consumers happily allowing "facility" and "selling systems" at Apple to keep them buying products at a higher margin.

Direct Application to Your Practice

Ideally, at the next remodel or refresh of carpets, paint, counters, and cabinets, think about improving every component of the practice. If you are years away from a remodel or refresh, focus on the areas that patients see during the consultation phase, and upgrade the surfaces in those areas.

⇒ The consultation room

⇒ The fee presentation area

⇒ The reception area

⇒ Any other area of the office that is restricted to the selling process

Having a well-polished system for gaining case acceptance and ethically selling your services can offset most of the negative impact that physical context can have on patient decision. Why let context sabotage things, knowing that your facility has an automatic effect on your end result? Why let it drag down results needlessly? You could see this as being unfair to patients. Some will decide to say no to needed care because something didn't feel right to them about the physical space when the fee is discussed. They may think, "Hmmmm, this seems expensive, and the office does look pretty, but it just doesn't feel right."

Key Tenet #33

Appointment Intervals Greatly Impact Larger Cases

Appointment intervals and their effects on case acceptance are misunderstood parts of the case-acceptance (Ethical Selling) process. Step into any practice, and you'll find dentists and teams presenting treatment in the same ineffective way.

Classically, dentists are taught during training to diagnose, prepare a treatment plan, and present a fee in a random fashion, even if it's the first meeting with the patient. Generations of dentists graduate and present care in this random manner, even though the majority will report that as the fee goes up, less treatment is accepted.

As the buying power of employer-sponsored benefit plans erodes (meaning less treatment is "free"), the benefits afforded to the patient are two cleanings, exams, and membership in the "crown-a-year" club. This further reinforces the way that treatment is presented by most in the profession.

As clinicians mature, a modest percentage will attend advanced educational continuums where a series of multi-day presentations are sequenced over 1-2 years and the clinician completes the series at considerable expense in tuition, travel and time away from the practice. As a result these clinicians will become proficient at more complex procedures. They often get "dental religion" as part of the continuum experience. Passion for dentistry is found or reinvigorated, and they go back to their practice to find that their ability to deliver services that solve more complex problems is derailed by randomness or the "all-in-one" (consultation-diagnostic-fee presentation) case presentation.

For too many, the result is complete cessation of presenting treatment options beyond single-tooth dentistry. For others, instead of asking questions such as "What's the best way to sell something that is complex and that is not enjoyable to buy?" or "Is there a science to selling, and if so, how does it apply to dentistry?" they'll continue in the same course but present to more patients knowing that, statistically, a few cases will move forward. Others restrict their presentations to phased-treatment plans in an attempt to solve the problem, yet they still wind up disappointed by the number of patients who complete such offerings.

When the concept of "appropriate intervals between Ethical Selling steps" is handled correctly, even without other more advanced concepts, results dramatically improve. Behaviors surrounding buying, deciding, and purchasing have repetitive patterns that can be understood and used to benefit the patient and the practice.

The intervals between visits play a great role in the decisions the patients make about their health.

For any but the most advanced teams, an all-in-one visit greatly stacks the odds against the patient pursuing significant treatment or moving forward with treatment options.

Here's why the "all-in-one" concept is harmful for doctors and teams attempting to treat more complex cases:

- It leaves insufficient time to build a minimal level of personal connection and liking.

- It ignores how much time is required to build trust.

- It creates stress for the patient related to money and fear of loss surrounding spending hard-saved money on something that will be perceived as risky by patients with serious problems.

- It leaves insufficient time to handle other stakeholders (husband, wife, significant others, trustees, children, other relatives).

- It leaves insufficient time for patients to process the information discussed and determine what they want from their treatment.

- It leaves insufficient time for patients to pool their financial resources and figure out how to pay and who will be paying.

- It leaves insufficient time for the patient to be ready to hear, and have a reasonable understanding of, what will be discussed at case presentation.

- It leaves little time for patients to consider their situation and qualify themselves related to time, lifestyle issues, money, etc.

- It leaves little time to review information provided by the dentist or team that impacts buying decisions.

- It leaves minimal time to understand the scope of the dental problem. If understanding of the problem doesn't match the problem, case acceptance is lowered, and it's difficult to achieve a congruency between the size of the problem and the fee required to correct such in the patient's mind.

- It leaves insufficient time for the patient to be ready for a discussion of price.

The ideal interval between visits, using a well-designed sales process, is one week. The one-week interval is consistently found in well-documented sales systems from a variety of industries. Member sales statistics and case-acceptance rates show that one week between visits is best for the short-term dental sales process as well.

The interval starts with the phone call when a consultation visit is scheduled. At that time, practice information and sales-oriented materials are mailed to the patient. This first-week interval allows materials to reach the patient and allows the patient to make initial, self-qualifying decisions.

Following the consultation visit, diagnostic, case presentation, and live follow-up/case-start appointments are set at one-week intervals.

Advanced Concept: Shortening the Short-Term Sales Cycle

The sales system taught to Academy members is the most advanced process in the profession globally. Any discussion of measures that fall outside the steps outlined in the Ethical Selling system (Maximum Case Acceptance) likely applies to only 20 percent of our members.

Two selling cycles go on constantly in a practice that is actively marketing. The short-term cycle is when patients call for information, some of them make immediate appointments, and they walk through the step-wise sales process with the doctor and team. The long-term cycle involves those who do not make initial appointments but who, due to periodic follow-up, eventually call and make an appointment.

Should you think about testing and tweaking the intervals and attempting to reduce the time involved in the short-term steps? Yes, if the components of the sales process that create trust (and speed of trust) are at the highest possible levels. These could include dozens of professionally shot video testimonials covering a full range of clinical conditions, complaints, and solutions, overwhelming evidence that the doctor and practice consistently deliver good results, third-party endorsements that are fully leveraged, and a high level of confidence at having mastered the Ethical Selling system.

It's almost a guarantee that any practice attempting to combine consultation/diagnostic or diagnostic/fee presentation appointments, in an effort to shorten the process, will have had years of experience in other systems, selling similar-priced goods or services (before learning dental-specific concepts taught at the Academy) or will have been fully trained and demonstrated proficiency in the Maximum Case-Acceptance System.

It is vital to remember that every step that involves tangible items (information/consultation packets) or the presence of other individuals (financial deciders) is even more critical when tinkering with the intervals and what occurs at different points in the Ethical Selling process.

When to Consider Testing

One of the signs that you can begin to experiment and make refinements to how you and your team structure the selling process is when patients travel great distances (several hours by auto or plane) and ask for a consultation, diagnosis, and presentation to be consolidated. Traveling patients are a sign that trust has been elevated.

What's the Benefit to Shortening the Sales Cycles?

You save time, because every hour counts in a time-intensive service practice.

Key Tenet #34

Appropriate Diagnostic Fees Help Patients Qualify Themselves and Boost Case-Acceptance Rates

The majority of practices seeking to perform advanced, elective procedures never have a basic understanding of the setup that allows appropriate fees for comprehensive diagnostic exams or the behavioral reasons for having a significant fee for such an exam. Insurance coding, borrowed (actually copied) from the medical profession, specifies complete exams and limited (emergency) exams but doesn't include what anyone leaving an advanced continuum would call a "comprehensive" exam or a "complete dental physical" in Academy terms.

The setup that allows for appropriate diagnostic fees includes fee framing specifically for those with serious dental problems being sought by the practice, discussions (written and verbal) related to how and why the examination will be significantly different and broader in scope than previous dental exams, delivery of promotional materials that show that the practice is different from all others, third-party evidence related to expertise and "category of one" status, and appropriate verbal skills in the staff who close diagnostic appointments.

Moving from a phone call to a paid diagnostic appointment with a substantial fee, without an intermediary, in-person appointment to build trust, requires more setup and is possible only through continued training in advanced phone skills.

The majority of those in the profession charge $75-$150 for an examination regardless of the level of complexity, which creates many issues from the standpoints of qualifying and the behavior of buying.

The services that may comprise a complete dental physical (photos, casts, charting, simulations, models, mounting, joint sonography, caries tests, cosmetic simulations, occlusal studies, computerized tomography scans, genetic tests, etc.) are seldom reimbursed under insurance schemes, and thus most dentists, having refused to learn selling systems, fall short of comprehensive diagnostic services. Diagnostic items that would give the dentist a better grasp of what's important to the case clinically, and that drive the development of predictable treatment options, are eliminated, to the detriment of the dentist and patient.

Charging what most consider a "substantial" diagnostic fee (greater than or equal to $300) accomplishes several things including the following:

1) It allows for a near break-even fee to be reached, at least for the facility operation and staff time expenditure. It is possible to create a sales process that allows for a true break-even diagnostic fee on doctor time expenditure, but for most, the best option is to build fees for "thinking and planning" into the case. By building diagnostic thinking time into the treatment, qualifying steps will occur.

Several years ago, one newer Academy member was busy diagnosing and treatment planning (including sequencing all the treatment steps) before financial qualification. It was impossible to have a starting conversation about what was needed, related to case-acceptance reports and photos at each case presentation, because the workload of diagnostics and "theoretical" treatment planning for every individual patient was already taking more than his available time.

It's known that 90 percent of those responding to marketing for complex services will not enter treatment in the first year. Your most complex diagnostic routines, which require enormous time investments, can be reserved for the 10 percent who are most likely to opt for treatment.

2) Payment of a significant diagnostic fee indicates how serious a patient is when considering elective care, reduces lost time in the practice, and helps eliminate finances as a reason that treatment is not accepted.

Free information about dental procedures abounds on the Internet. In the absence of selling systems that result in the practice providing appropriate information to the patient before appointments, it is easy to get trapped into discussions about treatment which aren't productive or an efficient use of the patient, team, or doctor's time.

No system for selling will mean that you and your team are at the mercy of the patient's random buying system which is unlikely to be rational and very likely to be based on their interaction with previous dental practices.

The higher the diagnostic fee, the more qualified the individual will be financially. A lower diagnostic fee allows many who aren't financially qualified to continue to case presentation, resulting in frustration for the staff/doctor and embarrassment and anger for the patient.

Other important qualifiers related to lifestyle/family/"financial other" issues and time should be dealt with as separate issues. Those qualified financially but unqualified in other respects will consume irreplaceable time.

A significant diagnostic fee paid as a "first transaction" makes for an easier decision at the next transaction. The higher the fee paid the first time, the more likely a more costly transaction will occur next time. From a buying-behavior standpoint, all first transactions in service relationships make for easier second transactions.

The size of the first transaction influences the size of subsequent transactions, a critical concept because all dental treatment plans are multiples of the diagnostic fees paid.

If the diagnostic fee is low, the far more costly treatment options seem unusual psychologically, and the automatic response is to doubt the justifications given for treatment cost, even by those who are financially qualified.

Key Tenet #35

Understanding Phone Price-Shopping Behavior

Price comparison is a routine behavior. Newspapers, consumer-rating magazines, word of mouth, or visiting multiple stores with similar products was the old-fashioned way to price shop.

The new way is online (pricegrabber.com, etc.). The even newer way is scanning the bar code of the item you are considering on a smartphone and letting Amazon give you a list of stores and varying prices.

Most consumers are one click away from finding a cheaper item, ordering on the spot, and walking out of a given retailer. Similar services are already being tested in the medical-dental arena and will be aimed at general dental services in the near future.

Price-comparison behavior isn't just for consumer goods. Patients routinely see dental services as a commodity and worthy of price-comparison shopping. It is hard to blame the consumer, because most dentists do a less-than-stellar job of advertising why their service, version, or mix of services is different from another office. Few dentists make any attempt to remove themselves from the "commodity game."

Promotional materials and messages at fighting commodity pricing are tremendously powerful. Examples can be easily found of practices being in close proximity, where one dentist struggles with a crown fee of $700 while 150 feet away, another dentist in the same setting charges $2,000. Major differences exist in the setup and accumulated advantages of one practice versus another that ultimately create the value of the service (beyond wishing to get a certain fee and getting it).

Some mass-market businesses you are likely familiar with who have avoided the commodity pricing game include: Saks, Disney, BMW, Mercedes, and Apple. Each company goes to great lengths to make what it does unique in the customer's eyes even though in reality there are others selling a similar produce or experience, transmit the "why" and "because," and as a result garner higher prices than competitors. The complexity required for a mass consumption business to create reasons why that justify their pricing in the customers' mind is greater than what you are tasked with as a professional service business owner.

Controlling Pricing and Phone Shoppers

Even with creation of non-commodity pricing and powerful reasons why something can never be low cost, phone shoppers will call your practice weekly, if not daily, asking for prices. A question I hear repeatedly is, "How can I stop having patients ask for the price over the phone?" The answer is, "When you get the phone disconnected."

The best solution is to defer by offering a consultation, get the caller's name, and honestly and emphatically explain, "Ms. Jones, I am not the doctor, and my job is to help you get in to see the doctor right away so that your best options can be discussed." It's OK to be honest about the fact that there are many treatment factors that can't be figured out over the phone. While some diagnosis can be guessed over the phone, beyond medication, treatment for any diagnosis is impossible to guess over the phone. "Ms. Jones, would you let your eye doctor try to guess your prescription strength or have a heart doctor diagnose a heart condition by talking to you over the phone? There's no way to understand your situation without looking at the problem."

Phone shoppers are notorious for asking, "Can't you give me a ballpark estimate?" The best response is, "Ms. Jones, I'd like to send you some information about the type of dentistry we do here. The doctor has put together some fee ranges, and I'd like to send you a copy." Move on to getting the address portion of the telephone script.

Should the caller ask for the "ballpark estimate" one more time, it's acceptable to "go technical" by asking dental-related questions about the procedure the person is trying to compare. This is the one time that technical complexity can help, because it illustrates why pricing is more than a single fee applied for all situations. When the caller asks for an estimate a third time, technical details transmit complexity and uncertainty: "What's your bone quality at the surgical site? Will you need bone augmentation? Would it make sense to do your surgery with a computer-guided method?" After the patient answers "no," "I don't know," or "I haven't a clue," you can return to "The best thing I can do is to have you see the doctor."

Bonus Advanced Concept

Academy members understand the concept of "appropriate discounting." This concept can be brought into the price-shopping conversation. For those with a highly trained phone staff, insert language into the "ballpark" conversation such as this: "There can be times when discounts for certain types of situations apply, and because of this, it is best to make an appointment to see the doctor."

Key Tenet #36

Understand What Every Patient Wants from You; How to be More Referable in All Your Relationships

"The great question that has never been answered, and which I have not yet been able to answer, despite my thirty years of research into the feminine soul, is 'What does a woman want?'"—Sigmund Freud

Compared to this question that seemingly perplexed Freud at the end of his life, you've got it easy when it comes to understanding what each patient wants, regardless of gender or whether the patient is referred by another patient or colleague.

1. **No pain.** It is paramount to have the right topical anesthetics and remove anxiety with oral and/or IV medication. For practices not performing IV services, having a reliable source for anesthesia services is a must. In this day and age, patients will pay a premium to feel no pain and to have no memory of treatment. Some will fly thousands of miles; others will drive five to six hours. Pain, or the lack of it, is that powerful of a motivator.

2. **Make complex things simpler.** We've covered how the complexity of life is increasing at a rapid pace.

When it comes to medical and dental procedures, the complexity is even greater.

Dentists who can take complexity and translate it into everyday terms with understandable, simple analogies see more patients benefit from treatment and choosing better options than those who can't.

Some dentists are not good at simplifying. Dentists with high fact-finder scores (8+) as shown on their Kolbe "A" operational test (www.Kolbe.com) can have problems with their conversations and complicate what their patients are trying to understand. If transcripts of audio recordings reveal that even with coaching complexity of terminology is not improved, someone besides the doctor needs to present cases to patients.

Everyone is looking for shortcuts in deciding and getting what they want in a world where choice and complexity are expanding.

3. **Options.** The patients want options, so give three options, four only under extreme circumstances.

Behavior studies show that as choosers, especially when given a long list of choices, we remember the first and last options. There's an Italian restaurant here in South Beach where the waiter runs through a list of about fifteen specials verbally. People remember the first, the last, and maybe an extra item from the middle of the list. Most humans can handle five to nine simple items for any sense (taste, touch, hearing, sight, smell) before they begin to make perception errors. Test yourself.

Choice overload and choice simplicity affect sales of everything. One recent study in a jam-tasting booth found that even with a large stimulus to purchase (a heavily discounted coupon), when a large assortment of flavors (twenty-eight) were offered, only 3 percent of those who tasted bought. When six flavors were offered as part of the tasting, 30 percent bought. This is a 3,000 percent difference in sales with something as trivial as three-dollar jars of jam. (Journal of Personality and Social Psychology, 2000, Vol. 79, No 6, 995-1006) The higher the complexity of what's offered, the fewer choices given. With dentistry, sticking to three options is best. With the most extreme dental needs, based on patient comprehension, dropping the choice to two options is a good strategy to help your patient make a good decision.

4. **Eliminate fear.** This ties in directly with the fear of pain. However, patients reveal other fears in interviews at consultations and diagnostics, as well as in the practice application, as long as someone is asking and listening. These fears include, "What will I look like? Will this really work? Is it going to fall apart too soon? What will others think about me? Will I be seen without my teeth? Will I lose my money?" The list of fears is long, and addressing them as part of a sequential series of steps at case presentation is a must.

5. **Respect and "guard rails."** Gone are the days when "doctor knows best" and patients were silent observers who nodded and acquiesced to doctor proclamations. There are plenty of physicians, dentists, and staff who give their patients little courtesy and respect. While that doesn't help the profession at large, it helps those who do respect their patients to stand out. Patients are looking

to you to help them understand what is appropriate in their interactions with you and your team and what they can expect before, during, and after treatment. Their expectations are akin to "guard rails" that keep the relationship on an amiable path. Setting expectations through written and verbal communication is the best way to have "guard rails" that keep everyone happy.

How to Be More Referable

One last layer rests beneath the items already discussed, and it plays a big role in whether or not beneficial clinical dentistry is performed. Think of this layer as the tenets that affect how others perceive you and how willing they are to continue doing business with you and recommend others to you. These are referred to as "refer-ability" traits, because those who have them get more business referred.

- ◆ Being on time

- ◆ Doing what you say you'll do, when you say you'll do it

- ◆ Saying please and thank you

- ◆ Apologizing when you mess up and making it right

In the past, these would be thought of as common courtesy. In today's world, these civil behaviors are absent from too many professional settings. Those who adhere to such principles stand out.

Key Tenet #37 (Part 1)

Patient Understanding as a
Critical Case-Presentation Concept

Everywhere you turn in the profession, renowned clinical teaching experts will help you learn to perform procedures and give you the sequence of what is clinically predictable for the conditions. The CE instructor will often insinuate that somehow, as part of an excellent clinical course, you'll know so much about "case presentation" that it automatically leads to case acceptance. No offense to Dr. John Kois, but a recent promotional announcement for his excellent treatment-planning course (which the doctors reading this book are strongly advised to attend), is an example of that kind of statement.

While the clinical concepts taught in the most highly regarded courses are powerful, there is little chance that what's being handed to the practitioner will result in a substantial number of patients calling the practice and asking for the clinical procedures which are added to the clinician's basket of services that result from attendance. Most of those teaching ignore this important small detail. Much to Dr. Kois' credit he readily admits that things like an understanding of marketing and attendance at case-acceptance trainings are a necessity to ultimately get the most benefits from his course and clinical teachings.

You can attend seminars on case presentation where attempts will be made to teach you "dog and pony show" tricks or to sell you on "whiz bang" technology that parades technical images in front of the patient, with the stated goal of making treatment acceptance happen. "Magic wands," "dental budgets," "if the patients says X, you say Y," and "handling objections" are consistent themes that run through these presentations

Academy members would go further in pointing out that laying the groundwork for understanding and ultimately deciding in favor of treatment starts when the patient is interested in the practice and when the items ("shock and awe" information or consultation packets) are handed to the patient for review, and what is or isn't said on the phone and at live consultations and diagnostic visits.

If your patients have no clue what you are saying (conception of treatment, disease, options for treatment), there is little chance that they will select treatments that cost significant sums and time, regardless of how well you know the procedure, the plan of action, the benefits received, or the losses prevented.

Once you leave behind fee levels where the patient can write a check the same day for the service, many other issues affect whether or not the case gets done.

Besides the sequence of events (discussed in depth in the Academy's Ethical Selling training program and Maximum Case-Acceptance System), some important generalities can be made about this concept of patient understanding:

⇒ Patient understanding ties directly to getting the most yeses from your presented cases.

⇒ Complexity is the enemy of patient understanding.

⇒ The more complexity you reduce at the time of the case presentation, through photos and word choice, the more cases that will go forward.

⇒ Dentistry is complex, and it's natural for the clinician to drift into complex clinic-speak. Dentistry that solves multi-tooth or whole-mouth problems is complex. It is difficult to become a "results maker" where the technology and procedures learned can be used to solve complex problems for a lengthy period. If you let the complexity of dentistry confuse the patients, they will choose to do nothing as a "fail safe."

⇒ As something becomes more costly, the process used to sell it grows more complex, but the language for selling it doesn't need to. The more complex it is, the more critical it is to simplify the language.

⇒ Most dentists, including your competitors, are "complexity generators." For those marketing for elective and advanced procedures, be observant, and you'll notice this. Patients will come to you who've already been to another dentist, recently or years ago, with the comment, "I liked Dr. Jones, but I couldn't understand what he was talking about, so I decided do nothing."

⇒ If the doctor's portion of the case presentation can't be delivered in twenty-five minutes, something is broken in your selling system. Attention spans are limited with any topic, and being forced to focus on something more complex than what's encountered in daily life further limits your patient's attention.

Key Tenet #37 (Part 2)

Confused Minds Don't Act; Unease Creates Inaction

As dental complexity goes up, the more obliged you are to prevent patient confusion over options. Two practices are located in the same city with similar technologies and levels of experience, and both possess advanced clinical knowledge. They both have pleasant personalities and a staff to match. In one practice, the clinician rarely performs the life-changing procedures that required years of time and financial investment. The second clinician, with each passing year, has dozens of patients who opt for the best that the science and art of dentistry can give. These patients offer thanks and testaments to the doctor's skill, and they pay fees commensurate with the level of care, skill, and judgment.

What's the difference? One clinician is highly skilled at explaining every procedure in exquisite technical detail to the patients. The other clinician knows that when a patient becomes confused about options, needed dentistry is seldom chosen, regardless of how beneficial the treatment is to the patient in their daily life. One clinician stays frustrated, never "connecting the dots" between the words that cause a patient's eyes to "glaze over," while the other helps more patients by doing everything possible to ensure that the benefits dentistry provides are described in a manner that is as confusion free as possible. One never thinks to record and investigate what's being said, while the other is highly concerned about such matters and does periodic evaluations.

Not only is the anecdotal evidence piled high, but there are fifty years of science from the field of influence and persuasion to draw on, and nearly half of those studies show how complexity directly impacts choice.

There will always be limits, even with the basics. Even before these areas of science came into their own, population testing from the days of the rotary phone showed that there was a limit to how much complexity and memory the average human can handle even with simple digits. Seven digits are the maximum number easily and routinely memorized.

Cognitive Load and Complexity—Both Up!

In the second decade of the 2000s, the cognitive load, while not necessarily requiring deeper knowledge than previous years, is markedly greater in terms of the number of different items that make up the topics of general knowledge. Technology crutches help us "remember" passwords and subject matter and quickly refresh ourselves on whatever is needed be it essential or trivial. There are more decisions to be made, more information to be taken into account before deciding, and more choices, many of which are complex and require experts to help simplify them.

Technical Advancements, Greater Cognitive Load, and More Choices

All these factors mean that the never-ending increase in complexity in the world around us, and that of your patients, adds to the likelihood that confusion will be the order of the day when anything beyond the basics is discussed in the consultation room.

Patients make poor choices that can easily be prevented if more average dentists are aware of the macro issues and know what to do, on the micro level, to help the patient decide.

Practical Ways to Avoid Confusion and Unease

Here are a few of the most relevant items pulled from the behavioral science surrounding complexity and choice. If you make these items a priority, you won't needlessly and negatively impact your patient's decision making.

- The perception of being in control reduces stress, unease, and difficulty with choosing. Anything that removes the perception of control creates an opposite effect (no choice).

- The more complex the treatment options, the more important reducing number of treatment options becomes. Limiting the options allows you to be the consummate, professional expert who navigates the complexity for the patient—one reason that fees can be above average!

- As individuals, regardless of logic, we believe we're more unique than we really are. Treatment solutions presented as "unique" for the patient's situation create ease.

- Anything about you, your team, or physical environment that needlessly creates a sense of "unease" reduces the chances your patients and prospective patients will trust your recommendations. "High-pressure" sales methods, still taught in certain quarters of the profession, also activate instinctual defense systems.

- Framing the choices offered with "avoidance of loss" as the focus decidedly influences choice. In studies of people choosing from life-and-death medical scenarios, people routinely pick less-desirable treatment based on whether or not loss is highlighted when the options are presented.

- Naming the treatment choices presented reduces complexity and simplifies choice.

- Extremely simple choices allow for up to nine items to be differentiated. However, four to six is optimum, even with simple choices involving flavor, color, type of widget, etc. Increased complexity of an item or service forces fewer patients to be confident and comfortable with a decision. For complex dentistry, professionals are limited to three to four options. Beyond that, needless confusion and inaction are likely.

(Author's note: Why Tenet 37 Part 2? Simply because "40 Tenets" doesn't sound as interesting to potential readers.)

Key Tenet #38

The Number of Individuals at Case Presentation Matters

Who is present at case presentation, beyond the financial decider, makes a difference. Hands down the absence of "the decider" is the most violated fundamental component left out of most practice systems for selling professional services. Beyond that critical error, not having an additional person from the practice present at treatment presentations, besides the doctor, patient, and decider, also negatively impacts patients deciding to go forward with better treatment.

Yes, I know you are likely asking yourself, "What? How is that possible? We've now put into place a system for getting the financial decider to the appointment, we have our qualified patient present, and we have our well-prepared doctor performing a stellar case presentation. Now you're saying that without the correct number of individuals in the room at the presentation, we're decreasing our patient's ability and comfort in deciding on major care?"

Correct. In the mid-twentieth century, IBM, a company full of high fact-finding individuals, undertook a study to see what happened when its sales force went to client and potential client offices and how much business was booked. Eventually a trend was noted in that a significant difference was found in clients opting for IBM services when two salespeople were present at discussions regarding options (the presentation) versus when one salesman was at the presentation. More investigation led to noting that this difference was present even when the primary salesman wasn't a "star" performer. IBM adopted the policy of having two representatives attend presentations. Why this impacted results is irrelevant. The important point is that any business adopting this principle gains another accumulated advantage over those who don't.

Everywhere you turn, you'll find a few highly skilled clinicians presenting cases with the major deciders there but not a staff member.

Why is this error so common in the profession? Modeling in dental school is one of the main reasons. "Who was taught in dental school to make sure that the correct number of individuals needed to influence decision making positively are at the treatment presentation?" When the question is asked in the lecture room, no hands go up. This lack of modeling, followed by years of repeating the same erroneous routines, results in not having the correct individuals or number of individuals at the presentation.

Even years after being taught the "why" and the "how" to make this happen, it's not uncommon to find practices being lax about these principles and seeing more patients than necessary opt for less treatment (or no treatment).

Who is the most logical fourth person who should be present? While any individual from the practice who is moderately likeable and interactive is an adequate choice, it makes the most sense that the financial coordinator be the fourth individual. He or she will move on to discussing financial options after the doctor's twenty-five to thirty-five minutes (as taught in the Academy's Ethical Selling System).

How does this person add benefits during the case presentation beyond the "IBM Effect?"

⇒ Confirms that the presented options are good for the patient

⇒ Serves as a trusted advisor. Patients often see the staff member as a friend or advisor at their level and may ask questions like, "Would you do this if you were me?"

⇒ Contributes to knowing, liking, and trusting, which helps the financial decider who, depending on the case size, may enter the picture for the first time at presentation. The fourth person is the "Ed McMahon" to the doctor.

The Financial Other as "Informed Non-Chooser" in Some Situations

When you thought getting the financial decider to the case presentation and having the appropriate number of individuals was all you had to worry about, recent behavioral science data, discussed by Iyengar, suggest that when there is more at risk (health or money), the involvement of the "non-chooser" in the deciding process is even more important. The "non-chooser" is the financial decider in most instances and a friend in others.

The data point to the fact that with the largest treatment plans, it's best to involve the "non-chooser" through the in-office aspects of the Ethical Selling process (initial visit, diagnostic visit, case presentation, and follow-up appointments). The more informed the "non-choosers" are, as part of the sales process, the happier they are with the chooser's choice. The happier this individual is, the happier the patient is before, during, and after treatment. The data for "non-chooser" behavior and happiness impacting the chooser come from studies of life-threatening medical conditions and how informed the non-chooser is about the condition.

Key Tenet #39

Understand "Takeaway" Selling

"One-of-a-kind item"
"Limited numbers in stock"
"Only 3 left in this size/color"
"Two consultations available per month"
"Limit 2 Orders per customer"
"Membership approval required before purchase"
"Expires on…"

These illustrate the "takeaway" as a powerful concept in motivating customers or prospective patients to take an action. Why does "scarcity's cousin" work?

1) We often want what we don't have.

2) We want what we can't have (or even might not be able to have).

3) The thought of something we have access to being taken away creates forceful action to keep it.

Have you ever had to wait months to see a well-reputed physician in some specialty or an expert who was unavailable on short notice?

Have you ever waited until the next go-around for a CE course because it was booked by the time you wanted to register?

What about that time (pre-Internet) when you went to a car dealer and found out the color and options you wanted weren't available on the models sitting on the lot? Did this create emotions?

How did you feel in these situations? Frustration, anger, disappointment, or sadness? The common, underlying emotion is "want."

You likely analyzed all the reasons and logically explained to yourself or others why it was OK to have to wait or be disappointed, but the underlying "want" was there and was almost impossible to dispel.

Your patients go about their daily business wanting things, some of which are good for them: health products, healthcare services, time-saving conveniences, living closer to work, or things that lower stress or rejuvenate the person. Plenty of other things are downright horrible for them. The list is too long to even begin!

Knowing that human behavior operates in this manner and that decisions are made based on this principle, ensure that the promotion of your services includes "takeaway" items to help keep the patient moving toward a solution that is beneficial to their health.

How to Use Takeaways

In promotional language, discuss your services and what's unique about the practice. In patient applications and phone discussions, talk about the types of consults, limited treatment dates, etc.

You can call this "takeaway selling" or simply ethically steering patients in the right direction. Either way, the concept is ignored by the naïve and embraced by the consummate professional.

Conclusion

The 39 Tenets discussed have covered a range concepts and strategies that may seem overwhelming when taken *en toto*. You've been exposed to a frank discussion about fairness that may provide a new understanding on individual responsibility with dealing with what is unfair to you personally. By now, it's unlikely that you will disagree that accumulating advantages in your practice that other dentist are unwilling to seek out or acquire is a good thing to undertake.

Now that you are informed, I encourage you to critically assess what advantages you are missing and to diligently to work to acquire your missing advantages either through your own effort or through enlisting the support of others.

By applying as many of these Tenets as possible, not only will you accumulate more advantages for your professional practice that reduce the unfairness you constantly confront but ultimately your use of the Tenets will result in more patients getting the help they need. I wish you health and success in your endeavors in our great profession.

Resources

www.Kolbe.com Operational testing. A better understanding of yourself, your team, and other personal relations.

www.SmileVision.net Dental Imaging plus "Try Before
You Buy" Veneer technology. Two musts that show patients
what to expect before purchasing.

www.PinHoleSurgicalTechnique.com Contact
LarryBrooks@BigCaseMarketing.com for special tuition
rates. Dr. Chao's revolutionary technique is a gateway
to creating an entirely new patient conversation about
minimally invasive perio.

www.KoisCenter.com Risk based diagnosis and treatment
planning. Kois Track - Course I and II. One week that
unifies everything you currently know about dentistry and
changes your thinking for a lifetime.

www.FaceLiftDentures.com Contact LarryBrooks@
BigCaseMarketing.com for special tuition rates. Cosmetic
Dentures. The edentulous deserve esthetics too!

www.BigCaseMarketing.com For more information about
the Online Programs of the Master Dentists Academy
designed to give professional practices an abundance of
accumulated advantages.

15111480R00123

Made in the USA
San Bernardino, CA
16 September 2014